BOARDS OF
THE FUTURE

BOARDS OF
THE FUTURE

To David Dalton

Dr Chinyere Almona

May 2022

To order additional copies of this book, contact:
Xlibris
844-714-8691
www.Xlibris.com
Orders@Xlibris.com
831510

CONTENTS

This book is dedicated to:
Corporate Directors who are striving to make
a difference in the boardroom, and
Corporate Governance practitioners who are passionate and
working hard to support improvements in boardroom practices.

FOREWORD

Dr Chinyere Almona is a seasoned Corporate Governance expert. She first struck my consciousness about a decade ago when I took part in an IFC Board Evaluation Certification programme which she conducted. Even though I was already on the Boards of two dynamic companies in Nigeria and gained substantial knowledge of how boards worked, her humility and rich understanding of the subject matter and her grasp and dedication to her methodology impressed me greatly.

Chinyere is one of those who are best described as 'understated.' If you pick up this outstandingly articulated and well-written book about 'Boards of the Future,' you will understand what I mean by this statement. She has a depth that is so well masked by her modest ways that you will marvel at the sheer originality and uncommon lucidity of it. Her vastness in the theoretical framework of Corporate Governance is evident, as reflected in her simple illustrations with case studies she developed from experience. She accumulated much experience working in versatile roles as an advisor, assessor, trainer, consultant, and she is now a key player. Her views are practically hinged on the Organisation for Economic Co-operation and Development (OECD) principles and standards that she is conversant with and espouses.

'Boards of the Future' is based on Chinyere's 'Five-Way Directional Model©.' She diligently applies this throughout the book's chapters, leaving no one at a loss about the relevance of this model and how it serves the future. She links the development of a 'forward-looking mindset' needed to build the capacity of a 'forward-looking board.' The Five-Way Directional Model© provides the framework, while the questions and checklists facilitate assimilation.

She is transparent in her analysis, stating things as they are and does not play to the gallery. For instance, she described her experience from PwC many years ago in chapter five. Chinyere had this to say, *"I invested time and resources in building a reputation-assurance service. Needless to say, it did not gain much internal support nor traction with clients, perhaps because I was not adept at communicating the importance of the matter or because the market was not ready for such a service at the time - or both."*

My opinion is that the market was not ready.

In bringing her writing home to the readers, her originality comes to the fore. A good example is her simplification of concepts for her readers. She used C.H.A.I.R. as an acronym to illustrate the qualities needed in effectively steering the boards of institutions. The book derives its concepts from universal principles, but her vast experience across the African continent also shines through. Thus, the book has both local and global relevance as it has original contributions that would easily give it a bestseller ranking.

There is no doubt that her objective in writing this book to meet the needs of executive and non-executive directors of large and mid-sized companies would be met and exceeded.

At the Institute of Directors, we have a goal alignment with the author, which is the professionalisation of Directorship. I believe that the utility of this book would go beyond the author's initial target as I am confident that future-minded directors across the globe, be they students, lecturers, experienced board players, mentors, or even mentees, would find it a great reference and companion. I unreservedly recommend 'Boards of the Future' to all who seek to be contemporary in finding solutions to board challenges.

Dr Ije Jidenma.
17th President & Chairman of Council, Institute of Directors, Nigeria.
October 2021

ACKNOWLEDGMENTS

First and foremost, I am profoundly grateful to God Almighty for the creativity and for being able to complete this book project.

I wish to acknowledge and appreciate everyone who contributed to my corporate governance journey over the years. Considering my thirty-year corporate governance journey, those who contributed to it are too numerous to mention. However, a few of my fellow corporate governance practitioners come to mind.

- Phil [Hedge] Armstrong, former Director of Governance, Gavi Alliance, and former Head, Global Corporate Governance Forum, under whose supervision the IFC Board Leadership Program was developed and rolled out.
- Ansie Ramalho (South Africa) currently serves as a professional non-executive director at KPMG South Africa. She was Chief Executive at the Institute of Directors South Africa (IoDSA). She was responsible for the successful finalization of the King IV Report on Corporate Governance for South Africa, 2016, as the King IV Project Leader. Ansie conveys the seriousness of board responsibilities and performance with such simplicity, clarity, and candor.
- Catherine Musakali, an Advocate of the High Court of Kenya and co-founder of Women on boards Kenya. She was the Chair of

Kenya's Capital Markets Authority's Committee on the corporate governance code when I supported the committee to develop the *Code of Corporate Governance Practices for Issuers of Securities to the Public.* Her palpable passion for and a strong mastery of corporate governance and boardroom work is commendable.

- Roman Zyla, Senior Corporate Governance Regional Lead (East Asia Pacific) at the International Finance Corporation (IFC), whom I worked with for nine years developing and implementing the IFC Africa Corporate Governance Program.
- Rose Lumumba, the Corporate Governance Officer for the International Finance Corporation (IFC) in Kenya. It was a pleasure to work with you on improving both the performance and shaping of boards of the future in Africa.
- The core team that supported me to deliver the IFC Board Leadership Training-of-Trainers program in many African countries under the auspices of the Africa Corporate Governance Program. These include Prof Chris Pierce (Visiting Professor of International Corporate Governance, Lincoln International Business School - University of Lincoln), Anne Molyneux (International Consultant at CS International), Brenda Bowman and Alison Dillon Kibirige (Founder at AMDK Governance Solutions Ltd), and Brenda Bowman, Adult Experiential Learning Expert, and Trainer. Dr. Mary Jo Larson, a member and former Chair of the Advisory Board at the Carter School for Peace Conflict Resolution of George Mason University.
- Olatowun Candide-Johnson, and Pamela Watson (co-founders of the Butterfly Coalition), and all Butterfly Coalition members, who are committed to game-changing governance in everyday interactions and institutions in Africa with women as the catalyst.
- Prof Alexandre Di Miceli, Founding Partner at Virtuous Company Management Consulting, São Paulo, Brazil. He challenges my perspective on the business case for corporate

governance and gender diversity, in particular, with impeccable research outcomes.

- Daniel Malan, Assistant Professor in Business Ethics at Trinity Business School, Trinity College Dublin. He was instrumental to my attendance at the fourteenth Workshop on Corporate Governance organized by the European Institute for Advanced Studies in Management (EIASM) in Brussels, Belgium.
- Escher Luanda, my Namibian friend who is relentlessly passionate about establishing good corporate governance in Africa. He is currently co-championing the African Corporate Governance Association, an Agenda-Driven, Cross-Sectoral Platform for Corporate Governance in Africa.

I also acknowledge and express my gratitude to

- My numerous corporate governance clients, that contributed to my boardroom experience in unique ways and provided fodder for this book.
- Fellow members of the Board Audit Finance and Risk Committee of Self Help Africa (a member of The Gorta Group), a leading Irish international development charity dedicated to ending hunger and poverty in rural Africa.
- Member institutions of the African Corporate Governance Network, which I helped establish in 2016. We have come a long way, but there is still so much more to do to improve African boards. Good corporate governance has a critical role to play in sustaining a stable and successful corporate Africa.
- Mr. Ikem Mbagwu, Chief Executive Officer at Cumbrian Consult Limited, for peer-reviewing the manuscript based on his extensive knowledge of corporate governance and years of serving on various boards.
- Dr. Ije Jidenma, the 17th President of the Institute of Directors (IoD) Nigeria and the Chairman of its Governing Council. She

graciously agreed to write the foreword at such short notice, despite her extremely tight schedule.

Finally, I thank my family and friends who gently and graciously pushed me to the finishing line.

PREFACE

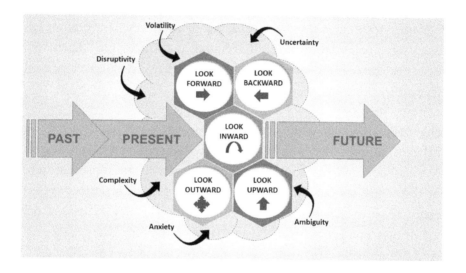

In 2017, the European Institute for Advanced Studies in Management (EIASM) in Brussels, Belgium, accepted my proposal to present a paper titled "Directors in the Age of Being on Edge" at the Fourteenth Workshop on Corporate Governance. The paper analyzed the causes of trepidation on boards as directors grappled with the consequences of the 2009 financial crisis. It is a well-researched fact that the crisis resulted from poor leadership, weak corporate governance practices, and a bit of recklessness at the board level.

Typically, Boards of directors and their performance may not be noticed when business activities are going well, but when things start to go awry, they are usually the center of attention. It is often said, and rightly so, that when companies fail, they do so mainly because of the failure of board leadership. Considering the corporate collapses of the past, boards must have a robust perspective of their stakeholders and the business landscape to create value for today and in the future.

My recommendations on what the board of directors needs to do to fulfill their strategic leadership responsibility were the highlight of my paper titled "Directors in the Age of Being on Edge." These recommendations were encapsulated in my proprietary Five-Way Directional Model©. The model's five distinct directions for boards are *forward, backward, inward, outward, and upward.* I explained how each aspect of this model must be understood, articulated, and harnessed to address contextual governance challenges that boards face based on relevant institutional peculiarities.

The model has taken various forms over the years and has been used in different contexts. The Five-Way Directional Model© is the core concept for this book and the basis for establishing the boards' preparedness for the future of board work. It continues to provide a perspective for leaders to focus their attention on what matters the most. I believe that boards that look and learn effectively based on the Five-Way Directional Model© will lead efficiently and leap exponentially.

INTRODUCTION

The Evolving Business Landscape

On March 11, 2020, the World Health Organization (WHO) characterized COVID-19 as a pandemic, pointing to over 3 million cases and 207,973 deaths in 213 countries and territories.[1] The COVID-19 pandemic caused global economic devastation, triggering unprecedented disruption to businesses worldwide. Boards and executives searched for answers and tried to adapt and innovate as much as possible. In addition, the ongoing megatrend of digitalization continued to affect companies' operations significantly. These factors plunged many company directors into situations that most had never faced before, and they had to continue to lead.

I cannot help but think that the best thing for boards to do in a crisis is to ensure that they are looking in all the relevant directions and making the right decision for themselves, the company, and the stakeholders. Directors' collective wisdom, insights, experience, and oversight are essential during a crisis or any change for that matter. Boards must seize the opportunity to provide critical guidance and support to the company, and they need to be purposeful in the directions they focus on.

In the heat of the pandemic, I published a two-part article on LinkedIn titled "COVID-19: Looking in the Right Directions for the Right Reasons." I based the article on my proprietary Five-Way Directional Model©. The article encouraged leaders to turn their eyes away from the catastrophic occurrences and purposefully look in the five specific directions. Doing this will enable them to take particular actions to survive the crisis and stay strong post-crisis. The business community positively received the Five-Way-Directional Model© as a practical leadership tool.

Board Leadership Directions

The purpose of the Five-Way-Directional Model© in the business context is to help directors focus their attention and articulate the concept of leadership, aiming to be effective leaders in the short, medium, and long term. The model requires directors to look intentionally in the right direction, learn from what they see, so that they can lead effectively and, consequently, leap exponentially.

Each director and the entire board need to

1. Look forward strategically, envision future business goals, and gauge the critical approaches to achieving the goals.
2. Look backward retrospectively and articulate the lessons from past experiences.
3. Look inward reflectively, perform a self-assessment, and take specific actions based on the assessment's outcome.
4. Look outward collaboratively, strive to become (or remain) stakeholder-centric to secure the license to operate.
5. Look upward soberly, discharge individual responsibility ethically, and enable the company to be a good corporate citizen in words and deeds.

Attention to these leadership directions allows the board to have a 360-degree view of the company, its stakeholders, and the business landscape. Having a well-rounded view helps the board be effective and efficient in executing its responsibilities over time.

The Vision

I have studied boards in the last twenty-five years and worked with various boards and committees as an adviser, assessor, and consultant. I have developed curricula for board training and general corporate governance programs for senior executives and led initiatives to establish corporate governance codes and good practices. I have also been privileged to train directors and senior executives globally as a certified IFC trainer on the board leadership program, including training trainers. Suffice it to say that I have seen the good, the bad, and the ugly regarding board leadership and effectiveness. Therefore, I am harnessing my wealth of experience to assist boards in professionalizing their practices to deliver more on their duties and responsibilities.

The target group for this book is predominantly Executive and Non-executive directors in large and midsize companies. They are especially in need of frameworks and guidelines that help them make sense of often unstructured, hectic, contradictory, and even threatening board and business dynamics. My interactions with many companies and their boards show that the scope of the board's role is ever increasing as the corporate marketplace evolves and will continue to evolve in the future.

This book provides boards with the guidance, tools, and roadmap to look purposefully, lead effectively, and leap exponentially, achieving sustainable business success. Each chapter presents five sub-sections that discuss the subject matter at a deeper level. Every chapter ends with *Quick Checks: Questions for Boards and Executives*. I included these questions to prompt readers to reflect on the concepts described in the chapter and reinforce the lessons.

Chapter 1 presents foundational information about boards of directors. Most of what boards should do to be more effective are addressed by the Five-Way-Directional Model© described in Chapter 2-6. I included some of the topical issues facing boards today, such as *dealing with crisis and digitalization*, in chapters 7 and 8, respectively. In chapter 9, the concept, signs, and consequences of dysfunctional boards are discussed. In Chapter 10, there is a deep dive into the dynamics of board diversity.

This book is arranged to help readers pick and choose (buffet style) what areas they want to focus on and enable them to surf through at their own pace. You may also use the book as a group workbook or checklist to drive group action toward greater board effectiveness. Whatever reading approach or style you adopt, I hope you take your board performance to the next level using the ideas offered.

My Five-Way-Directional Model© is an excellent tool for current and aspiring board members. It will help them increase their leadership effectiveness and improve their skills and behaviors in leadership competency, specific to their individual needs and the needs of their current or aspired-to positions.

CHAPTER 1

BOARD LEADERSHIP 101

The director's mandate to govern a company is a legal responsibility. This mandate, incidentally, is expansive in concept. The word "governance" is an English derivative of the Latin word "gubernare," which can be translated literarily to mean "steer." In this sense, therefore, governance could be adduced to a process of steering an institution. Similarly, governance has been described as "cybernetic," a description that aligns it with the ancient Greek word "kybernetikos," meaning "good at steering." This Greek word is similar to the Latin word "gubernare."

In another sense, cybernetics (according to its original application in mathematics) essentially refers to "the feedback and control mechanism by which a system keeps itself oriented towards the goals for which it was created." This is a control mechanism. Therefore, the role of the board in governance broadly covers both providing direction and ensuring adequate controls.

Different board structures and procedures exist in different jurisdictions across the globe to enable the practice of governance. Some countries operate the two-tier board system, which requires a formal separation of the supervisory function (upper board, composed of Non-executive directors), and the monitoring function (lower board, consisting of executive directors) as separate bodies.

The two-tier board system is typical for countries with a civil law tradition (e.g., France, Germany, and some Eastern European countries). Countries with a common-law rule (e.g., United States, United Kingdom, and many Commonwealth countries) operate the unitary board system, allowing executive and non-executive directors to work together.

This book does not differentiate between two-tier and one-tier boards because similar board leadership considerations can be applied, regardless of the board system adopted. In addition, there is a bias for the unitary board system, which is more prevalent in most African countries. Ultimately, a board "is charged with the responsibility of governing the enterprise and monitoring management." The Organization for Economic Co-operation and Development (OECD) corporate governance (CG) principles opened its section on responsibilities of the board with a broad statement:

The corporate governance framework should ensure the strategic guidance of the company, the effective monitoring of management by the board, and the board's accountability to the company and the shareholders.[2]

This overarching statement guides the detailed expectations of board leadership.

I will apply the analysis method of the 5W1H technique in this chapter to describe relevant aspects of the basics of board leadership. 5W1H is a technique that aids the understanding of a concept by analyzing all relevant factors. The 5W1H comprises five words that start with the letter W: why, what, who, where, and when, and one word that begins with the letter H, which is how.

Why Boards Exist and What They Do.

In his book "Start with Why," Simon Sinek explains why it is essential to always start with why. *Why* provides the impetus for engaging with a concept at a deeper level and inspires action. Therefore, let us begin with why the board exists.

A board is a formal construct consisting of diverse individuals appointed by shareholders to administer a business. In the book Corporate Boards That Create Value: Governing Company Performance from the Boardroom, John Carver states that the board acts as the link between owners and management, directing and controlling the company on behalf of the owners. Several academic and professional studies echo the same sentiment.

According to Pletzer,[3] an academic researcher, the board is the focal or critical pillar of corporate governance because it is responsible for monitoring its activities, setting its strategy, and appointing and overseeing senior management and the company's financial operations. These views are based on the agency theory.

The importance of the board is premised on the roles of agency and stewardship because of the separation of ownership and control of a company. Agency involves the transfer of capital from the shareholders to the control of management, and stewardship arises from the board's role as the guardian of the company's assets. The shareholders, through the board, delegate authority to management, and they rely on the board to act on their behalf.

The OECD principles state that "the board is not only accountable to the company and its shareholders but also has a duty to act in their best interests. In addition, boards are expected to take due regard of and deal fairly with other stakeholder interests including those of employees, creditors, customers, suppliers, and local communities." Therefore, boards exist as a connection between the shareholders and management, taking into consideration the interests of other stakeholders.

What boards do is derived from why they exist, and this is primarily determined by the Companies' Act and a company's bylaws. The OECD CG guidelines referenced above provide the remit for boards of directors, outlining the broad tasks pertinent to every board and the indicators of good practice.

Accordingly, the board should fulfill these key functions:

1. Reviewing and guiding corporate strategy, major plans of action, risk management policies and procedures, annual budgets, and business plans; setting performance objectives; monitoring implementation and corporate performance; and overseeing major capital expenditures, acquisitions, and divestitures.
2. Monitoring the effectiveness of the company's governance practices and making changes as needed.

3. Selecting, compensating, monitoring, and when necessary, replacing key executives and overseeing succession planning

4. Aligning key executive and board remuneration with the longer-term interests of the company and its shareholders.

5. Ensuring a formal and transparent board nomination and election process.

6. Monitoring and managing potential conflicts of interest of management, board members, and shareholders, including misuse of corporate assets and abuse in related party transactions.

7. Ensuring the integrity of the corporation's accounting and financial reporting systems, including the independent audit, and appropriate systems of control are in place, particularly systems for risk management, financial and operational control, and compliance with the law and relevant standards.

8. Overseeing the process of disclosure and communications.

Each of these can be broken down into separate elements. Besides, each board must consider its own situation and circumstances and what it needs to do to achieve its overall purpose. For example, small privately-owned companies might not be concerned with many issues that preoccupy large, listed companies.

Who Should Be on the Board?

The board is usually a balance of Executive Directors (ED) and Non-executive Directors (NED). The NEDs are external directors who do not hold any executive position in the company (although an NED may have an executive role in other companies). The main difference between NEDs and EDs is that the latter is an employee and serves in an executive position.

Executive Directors

The executives that one typically finds on boards are the Chief Executive Officer (CEO), the Chief Operating Officer (COO), and the Chief Financial Officer (CFO). Based on more than thirty years of boardroom experience, Walter Salmon insists that only these three insiders belong on the board.[4] His reason? As the business leaders, the CEO and COO communicate, explain, and justify strategic direction to the NEDs. Since the CFO shares fiduciary responsibility with directors for the quality of the numbers and financial conduct of the corporation, they should also have a seat at the boardroom table. However, in smaller companies, the COO and CFO might attend board meetings and provide information without being members.

In today's business environment, various changes have necessitated the onboarding of the Chief Risk Officer (CRO), the Chief Marketing Officer (CMO), and the Chief Information Officer (CIO) on some boards, depending on the industry and business exigencies. These directors are very conversant with the company's business and its challenges since they run the business and make decisions daily about its operations.

Non-executive Directors

There is no legal distinction between an executive and a non-executive director. They share the same individual and collective duties and responsibilities. Yet, there is inescapably a sense that the NED's role can be seen as balancing and challenging the executive director(s) to ensure the board functions effectively. NEDs are expected to contribute greater impartiality in their judgments. They also provide the board with additional external experience and knowledge and may have valuable contacts that can be used for the company's benefit.

Independent Directors

While all directors are expected to perform their duties with an independent mindset, an NED can also be an independent director. Independent directors should have no material relationship with the company beyond the directorship, which could affect, or appear to affect, the director's independent judgment. They are therefore able to assess situations objectively without the fear of possible retribution. The need to have independent directors on boards has in recent years changed from being desirable to mandatory. Most codes of corporate governance now insist on one or two of the NEDs being independent. Independent directors need to be advocates of sound governance principles and ensure that the board follows its principles. Independence is especially important when things are not going well, or the company is going through a crisis.

The OECD CG principles do not insist on the need for an independent director and indicate that

> *Boards should consider assigning a sufficient number of non-executive board members capable of exercising independent judgment to tasks where there is a potential for conflict of interest. Examples of such key responsibilities are ensuring the integrity of financial and non-financial reporting, the review of related party transactions, the nomination of board members and key executives, and board remuneration.*

The combination of new governance regulations and rising expectations makes serving as an independent director much more critical and demanding than in the past. The greatest challenge these directors face is to stay fully informed about the company on whose board they serve. Information asymmetry is often at the root of this challenge. When directors are genuinely independent of the companies they serve, they typically have limited engagement with the company.[5]

Regardless of the differences in directorship, board members work together to deliver on their responsibilities and add corporate value. The skills that may be valuable to the company can be highly varied and will likely depend on the industry and the company's particular circumstances. Therefore, it is vital to ensure that the board is composed of the right mix of skills, experience, and attributes.

Broadly, considerations for board membership should include the following:

- Financial expertise
- Relevant industry experience
- Legal expertise
- Representatives of key stakeholders' group(s)
- Honesty and integrity
- Diversity

Collectively, the board should have the expertise to facilitate effective strategic guidance and oversight. Directors should also possess sufficient knowledge of the company's core business activities, industry issues, and regulations. In considering these criteria, boards need to be of the right size.

A board with too few members may not allow the company to benefit from an appropriate mix of skills and experience. Neither will a small board have the capacity to form relevant board committees. A larger board, on the other hand, can make consensus-building both time-consuming and challenging. The board size should be guided by legal requirements, its specific needs, and its shareholders. Invariably, the right board size will enable productive discussions, efficient decision-making, and effective organization of the committees' work.

The Board Chairperson

A critical role in board governance is that of the board chairperson. The chairperson leads the board and ensures that directors contribute to the work of the board effectively. The chairperson's role goes a long way to ensure that companies get the best out of their directors. The chairperson orchestrates board meetings to the last detail, setting the agenda and goals for the meeting and coaching individual directors, particularly new appointees, to make an impact. An experienced chairperson knows how to redirect trivial discussions that do not have relevance to the meeting. A seasoned chairperson will also clarify issues where directors are complaining or talking rather than collaborating and working toward resolving them.

Most governance codes require that the roles of CEO and chairperson should not be combined in one person. Although previous versions were less prescriptive and recommended a greater representation of independent non-executive directors and formal designation of a senior independent non-executive director. There are two main reasons for separation:

(1) excessive concentration of power, and
(2) the roles are different and incompatible.

This separation may be inappropriate or too expensive for small private owner-managed companies; however, it is important to pursue as the business grows, takes on external finance, or brings in new shareholders.

According to Benjamin Rosen, the former chairman and former acting CEO of Compaq and a co-founder of Sevin Rosen Funds, "This (separation) is the single most important factor in creating the right balance of power needed for effective governance." American CEOs tend to prefer the dual mandate of being board chairperson and CEO. It puts them squarely in charge and avoids the likelihood of conflicts or power struggles within the boardroom. The downside of this model is that in the past, it often encouraged complacency by boards and discouraged them from getting deeply involved in issues until it was too late.[6] Most governance experts and some regulators prefer the separation. The split clearly distinguishes the CEO's role (to lead management and the company) from the board chair's (to take responsibility for the board and governance).

The Company Secretary

Another essential role in the board setup is that of the company secretary or corporate secretary, as they are sometimes called. Company secretaries have a vital role to play in the board arrangement and functioning. They are the critical point of contact for the chairperson and a central member of the senior management team, bridging the gap between the boardroom and the executive corridor because they have privileged access to both.

Every board member values the company secretary. Board directors know that the "go-to" person to answer their questions is the company secretary. If they do not have an answer, the company secretary will guide them to get the answers they need.

Company secretaries are unique as they are not typically board members and do not have direct responsibility for decision-making or accountability to shareholders and other stakeholders. However, they organize and attend every board meeting, providing advice and assistance to the chairperson, individual directors, board committees, and the board as a whole.

The role of the company secretary has grown in recent years, as has the reputation of the function. The role is transitioning from being a support person to becoming one of the critical governance positions. In some jurisdictions, their authority and position are protected by law.

The heavy responsibilities of corporate secretaries demand that boards appoint someone who is highly competent and who can meet the needs of the role effectively. The best people for the job have all or most core competencies of senior management and have a legal or accounting background. Good candidates stay current with the happenings in the corporate world. They are great communicators who pay attention to detail.

A competent company secretary helps the board to be efficient by introducing appropriate working procedures. They help establish and maintain clear interaction between the various governing bodies of the company and ensure that the board adheres to corporate rules and policies and all relevant regulatory requirements. In fact, in some climes, company secretaries are seen as the chief corporate governance officer.

Where Do and When Should Boards Meet?

There is a view that the main work of boards takes place at its official, formal meetings. However, a great deal of important board work takes place before and after those meetings. Engaging between meetings is important. The chairman of a communications company (and a member of other boards) stressed that "it's not just about the meetings. It's about being able to touch base in between meetings and staying current." Such impromptu discussions strengthen a board's hand on the company's pulse. Keeping board members informed also minimizes the background time that slows up regular board meetings. Nevertheless, the quality of formal board meetings can make a considerable difference to a board's success. Engagements between meetings should not detract from the robustness of boardroom discussions.

Board meetings are usually held at the company's head office and during office hours or at any other place and time that is convenient for the directors to attend. Boards are increasingly holding at least one board meeting at company locations other than the head office so that directors can visit the different company locations. The corporate documents would typically indicate if there are restrictions on the location of board meetings.

Virtual or digital board meetings are also becoming increasingly popular. Virtual board meetings allow each director to attend regularly scheduled meetings from their home, an office, or wherever they choose. Instead of reviewing notes after the fact, board members use audio and video-conferencing tools to join remotely and participate. Several digital board governance platforms exist to enable virtual meetings and coordination. (Read more on this in Chapter 8: The Board and Digitalization)

The board may elect to hold a virtual board meeting for a wide variety of reasons, including the COVID-19 pandemic and ensuing lockdowns, to accommodate the busy schedule of directors, achieve a reduction in travel expenses, or any underlying health concerns. For a fully digital meeting, all board members attend virtually. Alternatively, boards can take a hybrid approach, where some board members are physically present while others join online. Either way, the ability to hold remote meetings offers a wealth of opportunities for corporate boards.

Mckinsey estimates that in the near to midterm, most boards will continue to maintain at least a hybrid approach to their meetings, eliminating the need for directors to travel for each meeting. Following the challenges of the pandemic, there is a newly-gained comfort and satisfaction with virtual meetings. According to a 2021 Mckinsey survey,[7] the COVID-19 crisis has accelerated operational changes and more vital collaborations between directors and management that are key to a board's success.

The frequency and duration of board meetings depend on a combination of the company's maturity, the level of change in the business/market, and the confidence within the governance team to steer the company forward at and between board meetings.

Board meetings are typically held quarterly. Some boards have monthly meetings lasting three to four hours, while others have longer sessions every two months. Simple logistics may dictate that boards with an international membership are best served by fewer and longer board meetings. Generally, four to six meetings are likely to constitute an appropriate number of board meetings per year, particularly when committees meet between board sessions.

Certain corporate situations may dictate that the meetings become more frequent during M&A discussions or existential threats. Weekly board meetings are not uncommon at such times, with more frequent meetings often being held by specifically constituted ad hoc committees.

Another aspect of board timing is the amount of time spent on board work; that is each director's time commitment. Napoleon Bonaparte once remarked, "Ask me for anything but time."[8] Board members today also do not have the luxury of time. Directors are under pressure from activist investors and other stakeholders, regulation is becoming more demanding, and businesses are growing more complex.

One of McKinsey's global survey results suggests that the more effective directors meet these challenges by spending almost twice as many days a year on board activities as other directors do. Details of the survey results show that directors at the most effective boards spend an average of forty-one days per year in their role and say they have no ambitions to spend more time. But directors on less effective boards spend an average of twenty-eight to thirty-two days and say they would, ideally, spend five days more.

While there is no hard-and-fast rule regarding time spent on board work, directors should be prepared to devote sufficient time to get the job done. The duration of meetings should be tailored to the issues requiring board consideration. Ideally, board meetings should last no more than four hours. The chairperson's responsibility is to ensure that sufficient time is allowed to discuss complex or contentious issues.

According to a 2020 report by Heidrick & Struggles, with anticipated changes and expanding responsibilities, directors would be expected to devote more time to their roles. "The number of things on the agenda will increase, and boards will need to collaborate more with the executive team in order to cover it all," says Ian McHoul, chairman of The Vitec Group and NED at other FTSE 250 companies.

In addition to the growing number of items on the corporate agenda requiring more time, the increasing diversity of boards and the resulting broader range of views typically enriches, but also prolongs, debate before decisions are reached.

The objective is not merely to come up with the "right" answer but also to create a board consensus around the decision. Suppose a director believes that decision-making is unduly hurried or that insufficient time has been allocated and unrealistic deadlines have been set, they should discuss these concerns with the chairperson as soon as possible after the meeting. Indeed, the board's time burden is expected to increase so significantly that the existing system of holding periodic meetings could quickly be called into question and the governance model challenged.[9]

How Boards Perform Their Duties

The board performs its duties by having the right structure, practices, procedures, and tools. A board composed of talented and skilled directors is of little use if ineffective processes and tools are adopted.

Board practices or the modus operandi are mainly determined and guided by statutory requirements. Each board meeting is driven by the board agenda, typically put together by the chairperson and the company secretary with input from the CEO. In principle, there is no limit to the nature or number of items that the board may wish to consider. However, the agenda should strike a balance between reviewing past performance and forward-looking issues; and between operational and strategic matters (more on this in *Chapter 2: A Forward Look: The Strategic Board*).

The case for board committees

Board committees are an important structural attribute of the board, and boards function best through committees. There is also a need to delegate oversight of specific technical matters to specialist board committees. The OECD CG principles state that

> *Boards should consider setting up specialized committees to support the full board in performing its functions, particularly in respect to audit, and, depending upon the company's size and risk profile, also in respect to risk management and remuneration. When committees of the board are established, their mandate, composition, and working procedures should be well defined and disclosed by the board.*

The appropriate committees allow the board to

- Handle a more significant number of issues more efficiently by allowing experts to focus on specific areas and provide recommendations to the board.
- Develop subject-specific expertise on the company's operations, such as financial reporting, risk management, and internal controls.
- Enhance the objectivity and independence of the board's judgment, insulating it from the potential undue influence of managers and controlling shareowners in such critical areas as remuneration, director nomination, and oversight controls.

There are many different committees that a board may adopt. The four key committees, which large listed companies are expected to have and are recommended by most Corporate Governance Codes, are:

- Audit Committee
- Nomination Committee (or Governance)
- Remuneration Committee
- Risk Management Committee

Other committees may be temporary and established to deal with issues that arise in business. It is important to note that even if the board delegates some of its responsibilities to a committee, it remains the ultimate decision-making authority and retains responsibility for all board decisions. For this reason, boards should pay close attention to the committees' work. The committee is expected to report to the board after each committee meeting, making recommendations for approval.

Committees will sometimes need to consult with external experts on technical issues. These experts can attend the committee meetings, if necessary, without being members. External third parties cannot be members of board committees because they are not board members. Boards should also be aware that committees create a considerable amount of additional work for directors, managers, and support staff. Boards must plan for reasonable support of the committees since their work inevitably draws upon staff time and takes executives away from operational responsibilities.

The OECD ends its section on the responsibilities of the board with the summation that

> *Procedures should be established to facilitate access to information, training and expertise, and the independence of employee board members from the CEO and management. These procedures should also include adequate, transparent appointment procedures, rights to*

report to employees on a regular basis – provided that board confidentiality requirements are duly respected – training, and clear procedures for managing conflicts of interest. A positive contribution to the board's work will also require acceptance and constructive collaboration by other members of the board as well as by management.[10]

Board and Executive Relationship

As described earlier, an Executive Director is the one involved in the routine management of the company and is a full-time employee of the company. A Non-Executive Director is a member of the board who does not possess any management responsibilities.

The board and the executive(s) relationship is interdependent and requires regular communication and collaboration. Interestingly, when (non-executive) directors talk of executives, they often implicitly refer to the CEO. Broadly speaking, the board's relationship with the CEO is usually affected by its relationships with other senior executives and vice versa.[11]

Most directors understand that what transpires in a boardroom depends not only on the board's role, the approach that is implicitly or explicitly adopted, or on the board's understanding of the company. What transpires in a boardroom sometimes depends on how successfully the board builds a constructive relationship with executives, especially the CEO.

An ideal executive and board relationship begin with both parties clearly articulating the roles, responsibilities, and expectations. Then they must be committed to working together to promote the company's best interests. Overall, the board is responsible for setting the strategic goals and overseeing the execution. The executive director(s), including the CEO, are accountable for implementing the strategic goals.

When solid lines of responsibility are drawn, the executive director(s) and the board can establish a balance of power without stepping into each other's territory. Consequently, a formal delegation of decision-making authority between the board and executives, sometimes called an authority matrix, is essential. Factors that influence the authority matrix include the nature of the business operations, risk framework, and the board's degree of confidence in the CEO and the executive team. Overall, an effective board must ensure that the executives are accepting and implementing its decisions.

Inherently, there are some tensions in the relationship between EDs and NEDs caused by the nature of the roles. Executives may find it difficult to see beyond their direct focus on the business and its day-to-day operations. In contrast, non-executive directors (NEDs) may find it difficult to feel sufficiently informed about the daily pressures faced by the company. The executive director has an intimate knowledge of the company, and the NED is expected to have a broader knowledge of the dynamics of the business environment. The executive director may be better equipped to provide an entrepreneurial spur to the company; the NED may have more to say about ensuring prudent control. Despite these tensions, EDs and NEDs work together to create and enhance corporate value.

The board's relationship with the executive team has several other dimensions. One of the most noticeable dimensions is the provision of information. The board depends on the executives for a broad range of information about the business to be effective. For example, the board needs up-to-date information on the competition, customers, employees, critical strategic issues, and possible acquisition targets. The board requires that the information is presented clearly and concisely because its time is limited. The executives also need information from the NEDs regarding the external business landscape. Board members should share information that helps them make concessions, adapt to changes, address new challenges, and adjust to changing circumstances.

Expectedly, when there is a crisis or problem, the need for information becomes heightened. As one director explained, "I think there will be more demand for more information in particular areas when a company is being challenged. And the board members try to ask more insightful questions, to be supportive and helpful to executives in making their decisions. I think we've been doing this well at [company x] because the CEO encourages it, but still, we may have to put more pressure on him."[12]

The board's relationship with executives depends heavily on the board's leadership. This perspective bolsters the importance of separating the role of the board chair from that of the CEO. An effective chairperson helps improve the board's relationship with executives, providing a focal point for the board, and is a suitable information conduit.

While board chairpersons and CEOs need to support each other in so many important ways, both need to communicate and collaborate regularly and effectively. Board chairpersons and executive directors must be aware of board cycles, meeting cycles, and the annual cycle. The chairperson can also enable the CEO to raise sensitive issues with the board without damaging its relationship with him/her.

In companies where the CEO is the chairperson, a lead director can enable a constructive working relationship between the board and the executive team.

Quick Checks: Questions for Boards and Executives

- Do directors and executives at your company have a shared understanding of its purpose and their own purpose as board members and leaders?
- How would you rate your company's fulfillment of the tasks for boards of directors outlined in OECD guidelines?

- The diversity of perspectives that board members bring to the role can be a considerable strength for the companies they serve. How can your company make the most of it?
- As companies grow more complex, the demands on boards increase accordingly. Is your company's board up to the task expected of it today?
- Who should serve on boards, and does your board have a suitable composition?
- Are the existing mechanisms for holding directors accountable sufficient?
- How is the interpretation of directors' fiduciary duties likely to evolve considering the factors and time frame?
- Does your company's board have an effective process for executive succession?

CHAPTER 2

A FORWARD LOOK: THE STRATEGIC BOARD

According to the OECD Principles,[13] *"the corporate governance framework should ensure the strategic guidance of the company,* the effective monitoring of management by the board, and the board's accountability to the company and the shareholders."

The first dimension of my proprietary Five-Way-Directional Model© is a forward look, strategically envisioning the future. Boards that intentionally look forward have a *strategic focus* and are usually made up of capable, informed, strategic thinkers who can help take the company to the next level and keep it competitive.

> Leadership requires two things: a vision of the world that
> does not yet exist and the ability to communicate it.
> —Simon Sinek, *Start with Why:*
> *How Great Leaders Inspire Everyone to Take Action*

Directors need to spend a more significant share of their time shaping a plan for the company's future. There is a strong bias toward directors' fiduciary duties in the functioning of boards, which is fine. However, I have seen a desire and willingness to shift focus and pay attention to the future, which is more progressive. A leading company's chairman once commented that "boards need to look further out than anyone else in the company." He further explained this by saying that "there are times when Chief Executive Officers are the last ones to see changes coming." In a sense, he may be right as there are times when one cannot see the forest for the trees.

Boards need to have committed directors that are prepared for spirited discussions around the corporate strategic objectives and support the executives in delivering on those objectives. This is what it means to look forward strategically.

The Strategic Imperative

The board should define the company's strategic goals and ensure that its human and financial resources are effectively deployed towards attaining those goals. Based on the preceding text, it is clear that the board has to oversee the company's business affairs, and the long-term strategic plan is the most fundamental aspect of a company's business affairs.

Results from one of the PwC global Annual Corporate Director Surveys reveal that strategy is crucial for the future board. Studies of past corporate scandals and collapses have shown that the effectiveness of boards in fulfilling their strategic role by guiding strategy development and execution was lacking.[14]

Therefore, the need to be forward-looking is critical, particularly as technological and demographic trends are radically reshaping the global economy, making it more complex to oversee a successful business without a futuristic perspective. Moreover, as business executives grapple with the immediate challenge of volatile and unpredictable markets, it is more vital than ever for directors to remain abreast of what may be coming over the horizon.

The length of CEO tenures remains relatively low, sometimes three to six years. This short tenure inevitably encourages incumbents to focus unduly on the short term to meet performance expectations, which should be expected. In some cases, the tenure of the CEO could affect the ability to look far into the future. In a lot of these cases, therefore, only the board can consistently take the longer-term perspective.

The mismatch between the time horizons of board members (longer) and top executives (shorter) is a real challenge. The resulting lack of alignment can diminish a board's ability to engage in well-informed give-and-take about strategic trade-offs. CEOs themselves recognize this tendency to focus on the short term; 86 percent say they focus more on the short term than the long term[15]. A CEO in a board governance study said,[16] "The chairman of my company has effectively been given a decade, and I have three years—tops—to make my mark. If I come up with a strategy that looks beyond the current cycle, I can never deliver the results expected from me. Yet, I am supposed to work with him to create long-term shareholder value. How am I supposed to make this work?"

I have also met many directors who are seemingly distracted by the details of compliance and new regulations and simply do not know enough about their companies' fundamentals and long-term strategies to add sufficient value to the strategy development process. On the other hand, there are cases of companies with prudent, farsighted, and independent-minded boards that survive crises largely intact and continue to thrive. The directors of these companies are known to engage in strategic discussions, form independent opinions, and work closely with the executive team to make sure long-term goals are well formulated and subsequently pursued and met.

It is expected that the board should participate in strategic thinking and strategic decision-making processes, adding value but not infringing on the CEO's responsibilities. The board's participation makes the strategy supervision and oversight process more effective. In the article "What Makes Great Boards Great,"[17] Jeffrey Sonnenfeld alluded to the fact that the board's understanding and involvement in developing strategy enhance the board's oversight function.

Providing strategic guidance is still a struggle for some boards. This struggle was highlighted in the directors' alert issued a few years ago by Deloitte's Global Center for Corporate Governance; according to the report, many boards contend that strategy is tough to effect in a disruptive landscape. Others argue that it is of secondary importance, even irrelevant. Arguably, directors can delegate responsibility for strategy development to the executives; however, this does not absolve them from being accountable for the strategy. Therefore, enlightened self-interest dictates that this role should not be abdicated.

Vital questions have arisen over the years. What should be the appropriate board and executive interface on strategy? What kind of strategy process(es) will make the most sense? When and how deeply should the board be involved in strategic matters? Answers to these questions are controversial. Board involvement in formulating corporate strategy always has (and may always) be a sensitive matter in the corporate world.

The controversy regarding the exact role that directors should play in formulating the strategic plan of the company on whose board they sit will probably not end soon. The more involvement the board wants to have in the strategic plan, the more the board should be composed of directors who are well-versed in the complexities of the company and its industry, finance and financial structure, and relevant laws to contribute to the strategic planning process. In addition, boards need better information on products, customers' viewpoints, market conditions, and critical strategic and organizational issues to be an effective partner in strategy formulation.

A call for the board to look forward and step up into the strategy space assumes that directors will want to understand how the companies they govern adapt to changing business environments and take advantage of opportunities in markets (local and global). In addition, the board's involvement in strategy formulation makes it easy to address other board responsibilities, such as CEO performance evaluation, succession planning, and executive compensation. Companies suffer when boards do not spend enough time looking forward and scanning the road ahead of the company they govern.

Developing a Forward-Looking Mindset

A Mckinsey article[18] titled "Building a Forward-Looking Board" by Christian Casal and Christian Caspar suggests four ways to develop a forward-looking mindset that will help them better govern the companies on whose boards they sit.

1) *Review the business landscape.* The chairman of a finance company explained the requirement for the board to study the

external landscape to develop a forward-looking mindset. "As a starting point, we invite renowned experts and professionals in various fields—such as technology, regulatory matters, and economics—to board meetings, who talk about specific topics." In another company, board meetings are sometimes held in overseas locations where directors can be exposed to new technologies and market developments relevant to the company's strategy. The chairman of one telecommunications company says his board "regularly develops an outside-in view of the industry and business from public information. And from time to time, we seek outside advice to get an independent view on the firm's strategy and new potential development areas." This process is vital because strategy is not created in a vacuum and is rarely static. Instead, a strategy must evolve through an iterative process at the board level, considering changing circumstances, competitive disruption, and fresh commercial challenges.

2) *Establish processes and policies.* The strategy should always provide the context for proposed corporate actions, such as acquisitions, investments, M&A, and policies. A policy is among the most powerful tools a company can use to propel its culture and employee behavior in new directions and contribute significantly to the effective implementation of the strategy. Yet, most boards are aware of neither the complete set of company policies nor their content. Establishing processes and procedures that encourage or necessitate a strategic focus helps develop a forward-looking mindset over time.

3) *Consider the people element as an enabler.* Forward-looking boards are well-positioned to focus on long-term talent development because they understand the strategy and know long-term talent requirements. This understanding enables them to overcome some of the intricacies of appointment decisions, such as when divisional managers want to retain high performers even if the company's interest would be to reallocate their skills and

experience to another division with more potential for the overall benefit. In addition, many forward-looking boards hold annual reviews of the top thirty to fifty talents, paying attention to those who might eventually be suitable for critical executive roles.

4) *Keep an eye on the existential risks.* Every company must take risks, and the overall responsibility for risk management lies with the board; however, directors often overlook existential threats. These are harder to grasp because executives focus on the here and now, yet these harm companies to a far greater extent than more readily identifiable business risks. "Instead of only discussing competitive risks, boards should put in place a well-functioning crisis-management system" for cybercrime, insider trading, or corruption, says a consumer-goods company chairman conscious of the dangers of corporate secrets falling into the wrong hands. "We want to be ready for existential risks if they occur."

Effective boards will be those that constantly keep long-term strategies top of mind by always looking forward.

Building Capacity for a Forward-Looking Board

It is one thing to encourage the development of a forward-looking mindset; it is another to build capacity for a forward-looking board. First, consideration must be given to having a solid foundation. According to Casal & Caspar, referenced above, a solid foundation includes having the right directors who are knowledgeable about their roles and can commit sufficient time to board affairs. Further, board chairpersons would have to make an effort to include forward-looking components as standing board agenda items and prominent features on the board annual schedule.

In my work with boards over the years, I find that most board agendas require directors to spend the bulk of their time on quarterly reports, audit reviews, budgets, and compliance (up to 70 percent) instead of on matters critical to the future prosperity and direction of the business. Thus, for example, a board preoccupied with its fiduciary responsibilities typically spends its time on the following essential items:

Fiduciary

- Annual accounts
- Annual budget directives
- Next year's budget
- Auditors' report
- Audit-planning approach
- Audit committee reviews

These often take up about 60-70 percent of board time.

Strategy

Approve final strategy approach

Investment

Engage in the ongoing review of investment proposals

Talent

- Set talent-review objectives for the year
- Review top 30–50 people

Risk

- Determine risk-review objectives for the year
- Conduct annual risk review, including mitigation approaches

Decisions

Engage in decision-making, e.g., on budgets, investments, M&A, and key nominations

However, the following agenda items are what the calendar focus of a predominantly forward-looking board might include (in addition to the items above):

Strategy

- Set framework for the year
- Define broad options
- Outline/select options
- Approve final strategy approach
- Review strategic and competitive position, key performance indicators

Board Reinvention

- Conduct board 360-degree evaluation
- Determine the approach for board-process enhancement

Board Education

- Travel with sales staff, customer visits
- Visit R&D facilities
- Visit new geographies
- Inspect production sites
- Attend customer conference

These additional items should occupy about 60 percent of board time.

Recalibrating the board calendar and agenda to incorporate a forward-looking posture helps make strategy part of the board's DNA. Some of my not-too-recent experiences of boards and strategy have been of CEOs who present their strategic vision once a year, the directors discuss and tweak it at a single meeting, and the plan is then approved and adopted. As a result, the board's input is minimal, and there is not enough time for debate or enough in-depth information to underpin proper consideration of the alternatives.

I am aware that this approach is fast-changing, with some boards having strategic retreats. Boards and their executives require a flexible strategy-development process. The CEO-led executive management should prepare a menu of options that commit varying resources, risks, and rewards. This menu of options helps the board define a broad strategic framework jointly and efficiently. Then during a special strategy day, the board and executives will have sufficient time to debate, refine, and agree on a final plan.

An annual strategy day is essential and is now best practice. The strategy session should be held outside the regular schedule of board meetings, but in itself, this is not enough. Strategy, in its broadest sense, is no longer a matter for a one-day debate. Instead, the best boards seek mechanisms whereby outside directors can contribute their broader perspective to framing a company's strategic direction and purpose on an ongoing basis.

The chairman of a large transportation company described his board's strategic process and the board's role: "At the beginning of the annual planning process, the board's role is to help management broaden the number of strategy options. At midyear, the board's role is to discuss strategic alternatives and help select the preferred route, and at the end of the year, it is to make the final decision to implement."[19]

Engaging the Board on Strategy

Being willing to look ahead of the company and envisioning what board and management skills are required expands the possibility of appointing candidates with appropriate skills. I have read of leading companies that used this forward-looking approach to introduce a broad range of expertise reflecting its strategic direction and requirements. Consequently, these boards have top professionals with profound finance, risk, and general-management background and diverse geographic experience. Being forward-looking, these boards also have people with successful track records in their sector(s) of operation. Some companies need specific kinds of expertise to help them adapt to cutting-edge technologies or market disruptions.

In practice, it requires the art of balancing. The board's purpose and role are clearly articulated in alignment with the strategic business direction when the board is forward-looking. The familiar roles of a well-functioning board—such as approving the strategy, monitoring risk management approaches, planning leadership succession, and opining on the talent pipeline—may seem straightforward to list. But these things are not as simple in practice.

On the one hand, executives are sometimes sensitive about what they see as interference by the board. On the other hand, directors with years of experience and who are used to having a say are sometimes frustrated if they cannot intervene more actively or their views are not taken. Clearly defining the board's role and establishing boundaries help defuse these tensions early enough.

I read of a prominent investment company that creates work and role descriptions for the board and executives. These are reviewed and approved every year. The review and approval process always generates valuable discussions and makes the board and executive roles more explicit.

In the article "Tapping the Strategic Potential of Boards," Chinta Bhagat, Martin Hirt, and Conor Kehoe narrate a true story[20]:

> It's late afternoon in the boardroom, and the CEO of a major global infrastructure company's construction business is in the hot seat. A director with a background in the industry questions an assumption underlying the executive's return-on-invested-capital (ROIC) forecast that the industry's ratio of leased (versus owned) equipment will remain relatively constant. The business leader appears confident about the assumption of stability, which has implications for both the competitive environment and financial results.
>
> But the director isn't convinced: "In my experience, the ratio changes continuously with the economic cycle," he says, "and I'd feel a whole lot better about these estimates if you had some facts to prove that this has changed." An uneasy silence settles over the room: the board member's point appears relevant. Still, it requires a familiarity with the industry's behavior and economics, and the rest of the board did not have it.
>
> Finally, the chairman intervened: "The question John is raising is critical, and not just for our construction business but for our entire strategy. We're not going to resolve this today, but let's make sure it's covered thoroughly during our strategy off-site. And Paul," says the chairman to the CEO, "let's have some good staff work in place to inform the discussion."

This narrative provides insight into the importance of board engagement on strategy; a more robust outcome is usually the result. Pushing to answer the questions, as the infrastructure company above did, can help organizations enhance the quality of board engagement on strategy when that engagement must be deep and during the regular course of business. After all, ensuring that a company has a great strategy is among a board's most important functions and the ultimate measure of its stewardship.

Consequences of Not Looking Forward (the Hewlett-Packard Scandal)

Reading Krishna Palepu's *Focusing on strategy to govern effectively*[21] provided much insight into what could happen when boards do not spend sufficient time and effort looking forward.

Many companies strive to recruit high-quality board members with relevant skills and experience. However, there are boards with A-grade board members that are vulnerable to performing at a below-A-grade level unless they are deeply engaged with their company's strategy. None of the critical board functions can be done effectively unless the board looks forward strategically.

In the last decade, a series of occurrences at Hewlett-Packard Company (HP) provided proof of the consequences of not looking forward. Firstly, there was the highly contentious decision in 2000 by the company's board to acquire Compaq[22]. HP's shareholders narrowly backed the board's decision to acquire Compaq after a bitter boardroom struggle and an acrimonious proxy fight. This decision was taken shortly after the company replaced its CEO with Carly Fiorina, an outside hire. Carly Fiorina was brought in to deal with the strategic challenge the company was facing due to significant changes in its sector.

These changes caused a commoditization of a significant part of HP's business. Sadly, the company failed to respond to these changes appropriately. Meanwhile, two of its key competitors, Dell and IBM, developed innovative business models to deal with the exact change.

As the board of HP did not respond strategically to exigent external changes, its performance deteriorated. Similarly, the performance of Compaq, which it acquired, suffered. Less than two years after backing Carly Fiorina on the Compaq deal, the board fired her in response to internal turmoil and disappointing postmerger performance.

With the exit of Carly Fiorina, Mark Hurd, another outside CEO, was hired, the boardroom drama continued[23]. The bitter disagreements in the boardroom regarding the direction of the company continued. As the board struggled to resolve these disagreements, unauthorized press leaks of sensitive boardroom discussions occurred. In response, the board conducted ill-conceived investigations into the leaks that turned out to be illegal. This lapse, in turn, led to significant board turnover. *Chapter 9: Dysfunctional Boards* provides more context to enable an understanding of board dysfunctionality.

Although the company's financial performance improved for the next few years under Hurd's leadership, its strategic challenges remained unresolved. Then with a sudden turn of events, Hurd was fired for ethical misconduct[24], and another outside CEO was hired. The subsequent upheaval led to the departure of four board members and the induction of five new directors. HP's board again muddied itself in controversy, with observers and investors questioning the board's decisions and wondering about the company's future strategic direction.

Although there were several reasons for the upheaval in HP's boardroom, one of the root causes of the problem was that the company's board failed to notice, understand, and address the strategic headwinds in its sector in a timely fashion. As the board struggled to catch up, it repeatedly found itself hiring a series of outside CEOs. I doubt that any of the CEOs hired during this time was incompetent. The board just could not provide proper leadership of the company because they failed to look forward strategically and align actions to the envisioned perspective.

The series of events discussed here spanned a decade, and during this time, the composition of HP's board changed significantly. Throughout this period, all the individuals on HP's board were outstanding professionals with significant accomplishments. It is reasonable to ask, "Why did the board neglect the strategic challenges for so long?" "Why did a group of experienced directors - different groups at different times - end up with such challenging situations?"

The importance of a forward-looking board cannot be overemphasized in these times. Although HP is an extremely dramatic example, many great companies have experienced similar strategic failures. The corporate graveyard is littered with the carcasses of companies whose board lacked foresight. While it may be relatively easy to point fingers at these companies' boards, in retrospect, an important question to answer is "what can be done to increase the odds that boards can do better?" Looking forward is an excellent place to start.

Other direct and seemingly intangible benefits of the board's ability to look forward strategically include,

1. a *deeper understanding* by directors of the company and its strategic environment,
2. a *sense of ownership* of the process and the resulting strategy,
3. *better decisions* reflecting the broader array of perspectives,
4. *greater collaboration* between the board and management on other initiatives and decisions, and
5. *increased board satisfaction* and *more effective external advocacy.*

While the benefits can be significant, broader board participation in strategy requires a high degree of intentionality, and a well-designed process yields benefits.[25]

Quick Check: Questions for Boards and Executives

- Does the board add unique input to the development and implementation of strategy and contribute new ideas and knowledge of trends?
- Does the board provide a broad information base through a diversity of directors who test and probe assumptions in strategy implementation?
- How should boards and others evaluate corporate performance—over what time, from whose perspective, and by what measures?
- How much weight does your company place on the company's stock price as compared to the achievement of strategic objectives?
- Does the board understand the industry's dynamics well enough?
- Has there been enough board-management debate before a specific strategy is discussed?
- Have the board and executives discussed all strategic options and thoroughly debated the options based on a robust information framework?
- Does the board enable early detection of adverse developments and fast correction of mistakes through adequate strategic supervision?
- Does the board conduct a good selection process and provide intensive coaching to produce a high-performing top management team for the company's future goals?

CHAPTER 3

A BACKWARD LOOK: THE LEARNING BOARD

The second dimension of the Five-Way-Directional Model© is a backward look, retrospectively contemplating experiences and lessons. Interestingly, in today's fast-paced business environment, boards and executives are encouraged to continue pushing forward and never looking back (like the adage "forward ever, backward never"). In the desire to move full steam ahead, they give the act of looking back a bad reputation.

Looking backward is often unfairly associated with a loss of momentum or a derailment in progress. After all, the rearview seems less critical than the windshield when driving down the business highway. However, there is a well-known proverb proclaiming that hindsight is better than foresight. It means that it is always easier for us to evaluate past choices than when we have to make the choice.

Forward versus Backward – Striking a Balance

As I started to write this chapter, a book that I read years ago came to mind. The book is Todd Buchholz's *New Ideas from Dead CEOs: Lasting Lessons from the Corner Office.* Buchholz's book is an enjoyable but serious and realistic look at what we can learn from dead CEOs. The book was designed to help (or force) us to look backward, down memory lane, and catalog lessons in past CEOs' life and legacy. There is value when boards and executives look backward.

Warren Buffet once said, "It's more important to look out the windshield than in the rearview mirror." However, I have found that leaders who cultivate a clear historic perspective move farther and more effectively into the future than those who do not. A look in the rearview mirror of history could help boards that have had to deal with similar issues that others dealt with in the past, rather than being embroiled in scandals and cover-ups.

Winston Churchill believed that "the longer you can look back, the farther you can look forward." This opinion was validated by the research of University of Southern California Marshall Professor Dr. Omar El Sawy. He found that CEOs who reviewed past events before planning future events had a longer future horizon than those who look to the future without a backward glance.

Great leaders must be able to hold these dual (forward-and-backward look) and sometimes conflicting notions in balance at the same time. Looking backward can help boards prevent the same mistakes that others committed in the past. An appreciation for the past and an appreciation for the future do not have to be mutually exclusive. Although this balancing act can be difficult for some, boards that make an effort to learn from the past and understand the present and future contexts will make better decisions.

Look Backward and Learn from the Past

"Never waste a crisis. It can be turned to joyful transformation." According to Buiter,[26] this statement is attributed to Rahm Emanuel, US President Barack Obama's White House Chief of Staff. A period of crisis often offers excellent learning opportunities. Drawing lessons in real-time, responding to them, and reflecting over time on a situation are essential parts of the learning process.

It is often said that experience is the best teacher. However, this experience does not necessarily have to be undergone personally but can be learned through others. For a board to be effective, it must take time to understand where the company is coming from and what occurred in the past. Looking backward to learn from the past can be critical to our ability to contextualize new learning.

The first time I heard the word "constructivism," I dashed for a dictionary. Constructivism is the theory that says learners construct knowledge rather than just passively taking in information. As people experience the world and reflect upon those experiences, they build their own representations and incorporate new information into their preexisting knowledge. In summary, one cannot learn something new unless they can explain it using something they already know and are familiar with. Epiphany!

In high school math, we were taught to start from the known to the unknown. Applying past knowledge to new situations is a habit of the mind that is foundational to effective learning. Building this habit stretches our understanding, raises our standards, and prepares us to solve new problems.

The concept of looking backward and learning from the past is vital for me because I am a very reflective person. When I train boards, I facilitate a session where directors are guided to look backward to learn from the past. What worked? What didn't work? What can be done differently?

Earlier, I mentioned the book *New Ideas from Dead CEOs*. It provides such golden nuggets that can only be gotten from a backward look. Why did Ray Kroc's plan for McDonald's thrive when many burger joints failed? And how, decades later, did Krispy Kreme fail to heed Kroc's hard-won lessons? How did Walt Disney's most dismal day as a young cartoonist radically change his career? When Estée Lauder was a child in Queens, New York, the average American spent $8 a year on toiletries. How did she spot an opportunity to sell high-priced cosmetics and build a successful company? Looking into the past provides opportunities to learn about and from the challenges, triumphs, struggles, and failures of others.

There are several quotes by great leaders on the issue of looking backward and learning from the past.

- Pearl S. Buck once wrote that "knowledge of history as detailed as possible is essential if we want to comprehend the past and be prepared for the future."[27] Business leaders would do well to heed this advice.

- In a blog post, Gary Polson, CEO of Cydcor, said that the best sources for what works in leadership are the lessons of the past. He asked a pertinent question, "Why make your own mistakes when you can benefit from the lessons learned by those who eventually achieved greatness?"
- A wise scholar once said, "Learn from the past, or you could forget the reason you are in the current state." When this happens, the events of the past are likely to occur.
- A quote credited to George Santayana says that "those who do not learn (from) history are doomed to repeat it."
- Dale E. Turner tells us, "Some of the best lessons we ever learn are learned from past mistakes. The error of the past is the wisdom and success of the future."
- G. K. Adams said, "Sometimes in order to keep moving forward, not only must you take one step at a time, but you must be willing to look back occasionally and evaluate your past. Looking back lets you know whether or not you are headed in the right direction."
- Neel Raman offered this perspective: "By looking back at the past, we can intelligently predict trends and patterns and use them to move us closer to the results we want."

As an alumna of the British Council's Pan-African InterAction Leadership Program, I have not forgotten two of the eight assumptions of appreciative inquiry. People journey to the future when they carry forward parts of the past, and if we carry parts of the past, they should be what is best.

Another reason I tend to emphasize the need to look backward is the risk management implication of a backward glance. Overseeing risk requires boards to go well beyond their traditional monitoring activities and develop new ways of gauging the organization's pulse. This task can only be aided by advances in data science and computing abilities that allow digital compliance tools and predictive analytics capabilities based on past trends used to help with risk management, especially in banks and financial institutions.[28]

In the coming years, boards can expect increasing pressure to strengthen their risk-oversight capabilities while at the same time driving the kind of entrepreneurial innovation needed for sustainable growth and profitability. To do this, the board must look backward and become familiar with the past happenings in the company that they lead as well as look forward. Thankfully, every corporate board crisis in history has been documented and analyzed in literature and remains as reference materials for interested learners.

What Went Wrong

The debate over the role of boards of directors in corporate governance always intensifies during a crisis period, when things go wrong on a grand scale, as has happened in recent years. Many companies whose corporate corpses litter the industrial and financial landscape were deemed to have been undermined by negligent, overoptimistic, or ill-informed boards before the crisis. Not surprisingly, after every major crisis, there is always a renewed focus on improved corporate governance (better structures, more rigorous checks, and balances, and greater independence by non-executives).

Before the institution of any corporate governance improvement, after a crisis, regulators and corporate governance proponents are generally good at asking the question, "what went wrong?" Whenever this question is asked, the board will immediately scramble around to decipher what transpired and who is to blame and find scapegoats among the executives. This is natural following a devastating crisis because organizations (and their leaders) need to know what happened, learn lessons, and bring those responsible to account.

Understandably, from a practical perspective, a backward look and retrospective analysis can be difficult for most directors because it will often mean that the board was in a way complicit in what went wrong. Still, it is so important not to waste a crisis.

Unfortunately, despite the pro-governance speech by virtually all companies after the financial crises from the earlier 2000s, most of them still see corporate governance as a mere checklist of recommended practices. Following the corporate collapses at the beginning of the 2000s, Hamilton & Micklethwait[29] conducted an in-depth study to identify the causes of failures.

They believed that a thorough understanding of what went wrong is essential if boards are not to repeat past mistakes. According to them, the reasons companies fail are few and familiar to most, irrespective of industry or geography. The leading causes of failure were found to be classified into six categories, namely,

1. Ineffective boards of directors
2. Dominant CEOs
3. Poor strategic decisions
4. Overexpansion and ill-judged acquisitions
5. Greed, hubris, and a desire for power
6. Failure of internal controls at all levels from the top downwards

Another wave of corporate governance crisis starting from about 2007 gave the impression that the corporate world and directors did not learn (m)any lessons from the previous corporate failures. This impression was borne out of the fact that most of the companies involved in the 2007-2009 wave of corporate scandals presented the same governance problems of the previous cases from earlier in the decade.[30] It was abundantly clear that corporate leaders had learned nothing from the series of high-profile disasters. This is, sadly, the type of omissions that have led to history repeating itself so dramatically.

Let us take a closer look at the first two factors listed above, (1) ineffective boards of directors and (2) dominant CEOs.

Regarding ineffective boards, the challenge is often with the board's composition, structure, and practices. Historically, there is also a lack of genuinely independent directors. An independent board should provide a nonpartisan judgment of senior management's actions and strategic proposals and look after all stakeholders' interests. The directors may not do this effectively if they are financially beholden to the company (other than by way of proper compensation for work as a director), as their judgment might well be clouded. Let's look back into the not-too-distant past. We will discover that previous corporate collapses were caused by the fact that many so-called independent directors may not have been so independent after all.

At WorldCom, many of the directors came from companies it had acquired and owed much of their wealth to Bernie Ebbers, the co-founder and CEO of WorldCom. At Tyco, some of the "independent" directors either depended indirectly on Tyco for the bulk of their income or had benefited from the use of company assets at the discretion of the CEO Kozlowski. I find these same lapses on boards in most emerging markets.

Many boards fail to question the executives, fail to assess the competence and character of the executives, rubber-stamp decisions, spend as little time as possible in board meetings, allow executive compensation to spiral out of control, and accept management figures and explanations without serious questions. This happened at WorldCom, Enron, Marconi, Ahold, Parmalat, Swissair, and Tyco, and boards must consciously learn from these occurrences (more of this in chapter 9, where I discuss dysfunctional boards).

Regarding the case of a dominant or an overbearing CEO, this person is either a founder/CEO or emerged after a period of successful management of the company. The result is that the company invariably becomes packed with like-minded executives who owe their position to the CEO and are reluctant to challenge his/her judgment. This is combined with a complacent board, lulled by past achievements, which stops scrutinizing detailed performance indicators and falls into the habit of rubber-stamping the CEO's decisions.

There would seem to be a consensus that the CEO's competence, commitment, and charisma have contributed to the previous success; therefore, he/she is infallible. With no challengers or critics within the board, the CEO begins, perhaps unconsciously, to behave as though he/she is infallible and invincible. Shareholders and the board become irrelevant and a nuisance. This is the recipe for a crash. Boards need to take cognizance of the warning signs of a dominant CEO by looking backward into past occurrences.

There are so many articles and books written on the causes of the global financial crisis. Therefore, boards must understand how the failure to look backward and learn can contribute to a corporate loss. Sadly, over the years, I have found out that the past often shows up in the present without any disguise. Boards make the same mistakes that other boards have made in the past. Sometimes they repeat the same mistakes that they made before. One wonders why this occurs.

Reading through a blog post, *Why Don't Leaders Learn from History?* and the perspectives and reflections on the discussion thread provided some insight. One of the comments read, "I think the repetition of history by those who are repeating it is caused primarily by people viewing their own circumstances as somehow different from those circumstances faced by people in the past. When the decision-makers want to go in a particular direction, they rationalize away the similarities with historical events, perhaps often attributing the differences to their capabilities."

Another comment read, "Leaders often fail to consider history because they have an unhealthy sense of their own uniqueness, and they have a sense that the events around them are 'peculiar' to their time and therefore history is of little value."

The ability to appropriately balance the past and the present is what distinguishes great leaders from the pack.

How Looking Backward Can Help You Leap Forward

Kathy Davanzo and Dr. Jim Sartain, principal partners of CODA Partners, Inc., wrote an article[31] on how looking backward can help one lead forward. According to the duo, there are three important ways that looking backward can extend the horizon for a director or senior executive and those that they lead:

1. *Look backward and reflect on the journey so far.* Directors and executives can inspire change when they look backward and tell the story of how far they and the people they lead have come, providing evidence of the progress to date. This inspires progress, as whatever challenges may lie ahead becomes less daunting and easy to overcome. Good leaders highlight past accomplishments as a way of building collective confidence about the future.

   A certain company faced an uncertain future, was struggling with soaring debt, was unclear about its direction, and was not prepared for the market's shifting demands. They hired a new CEO to lead the change agenda and help improve the business performance and outlook. Within a few short years, this CEO used his ability to look simultaneously to the past (backward) and to the future (forward) to reposition the institution for an unprecedented period of success.

Early in his tenure, he convinced the board, senior executives, and staff to take a risk, as he guided the company to become one of the first entrants in the emerging market of a new service offering. The move was slightly unorthodox, complicated, and required a bold reimagining of the nature of stakeholders' engagement. Some challenges included an aggressive implementation timeline that appeared to be unachievable and a budget that felt unaffordable.

This CEO persevered, rallying everyone, and at every opportunity, he reminded them of the changes they had made in just his first year. He showed the charts and told the stories of the gains they had already made together at every opportunity. At every chance, he talked about how they were achieving stretch goals previously deemed unachievable. He helped them look back at every opportunity, thereby reinforcing that they could meet each new challenge, just as they had met the challenges of their recent past. It worked.

2. *Look backward and appreciate the efforts of the past.* Gaining commitment to a future direction is easier when the leader pauses to look backward and honors the past efforts. It is a validation of prior vision, effort, perseverance, and strategy that provides an opportunity even to consider a new pathway for success. Sometimes new directors or executives enter struggling organizations as diagnosticians. They are myopically focused on what is wrong and what needs repair, and they become cavalier in the broad brush they use to remind stakeholders where they are failing or failed. Understandably, conversations can eventually address deficiencies, but focusing first on examples of past choices that led to success can remind people that they can win again.

A prominent human services organization hired a new chief operating officer (COO) from a competitor to help lead the necessary changes to bring the organization's services and programs into compliance with new regulatory and accreditation standards. In the first few days on the job, the new COO held meetings with managers and department heads. He revealed his independent observations of what was wrong with their functional areas of responsibility. There was no discussion, only a list of failings presented with a thinly veiled dose of contempt for those leaders and their decisions. He was exasperated by their choices but did not take the time to investigate the context of those decisions or to learn that they represented significant improvements over the decisions made by their predecessors. In short, he failed to appreciate the efforts of the past; he indicted it and, in doing so, invalidated the effort and judgment of every existing leader in the organization. As a result, he could never galvanize the commitment he needed from them to be successful.

3. *Look backward and create a connection between the past and the future.* Many experts, such as William Bridges,[32] an American author, speaker, and organizational consultant, have documented that individuals, teams, and organizations may hold back from fully embracing a future vision because they sense a loss. Perhaps they cannot see a role for themselves in the future, or maybe they fear what they value will no longer be respected.

William Bridges emphasized the importance of understanding transitions as a key for organizations to succeed in making changes. He says that transition is the psychological process of adapting to change. Leaders who acknowledge people's past roles and efforts in the organization and the values that define them tend to open the door. Leaders who help individuals, teams, and organizations see a role for themselves in that future and show how they will remain valued will inspire them to walk through that door.

An excellent example of this kind of leader is the late U.S. president Abraham Lincoln. Nearly one and a half years before the end of the Civil War, at a time when the country's future was in peril, Lincoln cast a resonating vision and challenged all Americans to assume a role in, a responsibility for, ensuring, as he said in his Gettysburg Address, "that this government of the people, by the people, for the people, shall not perish from the earth."

But before he spoke of the future ahead, he looked back, speaking of the past and highlighting the values on which America was built. He began the address with the statement, "Four score and seven years ago our fathers brought forth, upon this continent, a new nation, conceived in liberty, and dedicated to the proposition that all men are created equal."

In this way, Lincoln inspired commitment by linking the future to the past. He assigned all listeners a responsibility and helped them see that by accepting his challenge, they, too, would be honoring not only the fallen but also the past they so strongly valued.

Looking backward is helpful if one does not take up residence in the past. Bring forward with you whatever helps sustain what is important and supports the future you aspire to. By cultivating and contextualizing the lesson of the past with your present and anticipated challenges, every director and executive can discover how best to move forward.

Repositioning the Board

A learning board understands that education is essential for successful boards of directors. To avoid taking up residence in the past, the board must reposition itself and consciously step away from the past. Particularly after a crisis or a challenging period, periodically ask and respond to the question, "What will we do differently now?"

Being able to step away from the past requires continuous improvement and continuous learning. Sometimes boards pay attention to the constant improvement of processes and procedures but neglect continuous learning (or do not consider it necessary) for themselves at the board level.

The ever-changing quality of the marketplace today requires that boards look backward and recognize the gap between the past and present, and be keen to reposition themselves through appropriate learning initiatives. These boards will continually evolve and grow to meet the present and future needs of the company, regardless of prevalent conditions. When boards look backward and reflect on where they have been and what they have been through, they consciously step away from the past and possibly outdated practices.

This constant evolution calls the board to go above and beyond the duties and responsibilities they are used to. For this evolution to occur smoothly, the board could establish a formal board learning process.

The best board learning or development initiatives occur when a specific person or committee takes ownership of the process. Typically, the governance committee handles this with the support of the company secretary. In some cases, it is the company secretary who takes charge. Some boards opt to go through a certification process, but this is not yet a widespread approach.

I have seen boards put directors' training very low on the priority list to focus on immediate issues. More successful boards make continuous board training and development a priority. However, ignoring the growth of board members, the process that will enable them to step away from the past is shortsighted and can hinder a board's long-term success. Board education should be structured so that boards receive quality training, at least annually.

The next chapter will describe the board assessment process, which should also trigger new learning opportunities. Board training must be contextualized to achieve the desired objective: to reposition the board for enhanced performance. Boards of the future cannot afford to get stuck in the past. But they must intentionally use the past as a springboard into the future.

Quick Check: Questions for Boards and Executives

- Can your company's board be described as a learning board?
- Does your board have the structures, processes, and information needed to carry out its oversight responsibilities?
- Companies and boards are increasingly called on to provide more and better information about their past activities, but how much and what types of reporting and disclosure are optimal?
- What should companies, boards, and their advisers disclose, and what standards should govern those disclosures?
- Does your board have a structured way to mine lessons from corporate history? Are these lessons formally articulated and shared?
- How does the board capture historical information on corporate successes and failures?
- How is the risk management process enhanced by looking backward to understand past events and trends?

CHAPTER 4

AN INWARD LOOK: THE SELF-AWARE BOARD

Look inward, reflectively, and perform a self-assessment.

An inward look is the third dimension of the proprietary Five-Way-Directional Model©. An inward look is a synonym for self-examination, self-appraisal, self-assessment, or self-evaluation. Looking inward requires a deliberate effort to be aware of oneself, judge oneself, and make critical adjustments as may be necessary.

To be successful, a company needs to have competent individuals on its board and management team who possess the right skills and work seamlessly together to align with its strategic direction. To remain competent, boards need to look inward and aspire to more "meta" practices, deliberating about the board processes to remove biases from decisions.[33]

In looking inward, boards need to consider the internal workings of the company on whose board they sit. It is equally important to conduct a periodic assessment of the board's overall performance. Investors, regulators, other company stakeholders, and governance experts challenge boards to examine and explain board performance and composition. Indeed, many stakeholders note board effectiveness and composition as a top priority and foundation for long-term value creation and sustainability. An inward look is a new mantra, and continuous improvement is the goal.

The Soft Underbelly of Board Oversight

A critical aspect of looking inward is the ability of directors and executives to intentionally pay attention to how they are spending their time and what they are looking at. What are the topics and issues that matter? As boards take charge of how they work, they must also take charge of what the board is working on because what they focus on gives a clue to the executives about what is critical.[34] The board can broaden its oversight role to include an assessment of the drivers of business health; it helps executives be more inward-looking and focus on critical internal issues. The board's monitoring can then add significant value.[35]

Boards need to train themselves to look inward at the things that matter to the business that they are overseeing. The book *Boards That Deliver: Advancing Corporate Governance from Compliance to Competitive Advantage* by Ram Charan,[36] a world-renowned business adviser, provides clear insight. Charan encourages boards to consider the *ten questions every director should ask.* This is a set of questions that explores the internal arrangement for which the board is responsible and could potentially make or break the company. Directors and executives should, but often do not, know the answers to these questions. These questions should enable directors to think about the issues that constitute the board's real work.

Asking and answering these ten questions is at the heart of taking a good look inward. Such inward-looking questions unearth essential insights that need to be brought to light and explored further.

1. *Does the board have the right CEO/executive(s)?* How might the board support further improvements if they are comfortable with the CEO and executive(s)? On the other hand, what should the board do if directors have any reservations about the CEO and executive(s)?

2. *How well is the CEO's compensation linked to actual performance?* The board must be clear on how the CEO's compensation reflects both the board's philosophy and the company's actual performance. Is performance measurement clear? Will the compensation plan encourage the right behaviors?

3. *Is there a collective understanding of the moneymaking recipe in the business strategy?* In Chapter 2, I explained the need for the board to be forward-looking and involved in strategy-setting. It is further essential that directors understand how the company's strategy translates into cash. A collective understanding of how a company, a division, or a significant product category makes money is crucial.

4. *Are the executives looking at external trends and identifying the opportunities and threats presented?* While this is a forward-looking element, the board is meant to look inward at their internal process to ensure adequate oversight of the strategy. How well is the board in tune and contributing to the detection of these patterns?

5. *What are the sources of organic growth?* Is the board comfortable that the CEO's growth plan is grounded in reality, not wishful thinking? Have the executives reviewed the growth plan with the board and kept the board up to date on progress? Is the envisaged growth delivering success, stability, and sustainability?

6. *How rigorous is the process for succession planning?* How comfortable is the board with the criteria based on which leaders are selected, promoted, and developed? How often does the board review these criteria? Is the board comfortable with the succession planning policy and process?

7. *Does the board have the right approach to assessing the company's financial health?* Cash is king and a good indicator of a company's health. Tracking cash is the best way to see how the various parts of the business work together. Where is cash flowing from within the business? Where is cash flowing to? How do the inflows and outflows work together to create value? The board needs to be comfortable with the cash flow trajectory and its implication for survival.

8. *Is the board examining measures that capture the root causes of performance?* How well does the board understand the premise behind each performance measure? How do the measures compare with the competition and in the context of macro factors, such as changes in the economy?

9. *Does the board get bad news from the executives in time and unembellished?* The board needs to hear the bad news—promptly. It is a tragedy when board members receive unpleasant information about their company in the news. Are the executives

sharing bad news with the board? If not, why not? If so, is there a plan to address the bad news, and is it credible?

10. *How productive are executive sessions?* The board can make the CEO more effective, or it can dilute the power of the CEO. Is the board coming to a consensus viewpoint on the most critical issues? How accurate and precise is the feedback given to the CEO? How constructive and valuable is the feedback? What has been the CEO's response and follow-through?

Looking inward and pondering these ten questions allows the board to reflect and recalibrate, which is necessary to remain effective and add value. This reflective approach signals that the board is on top of its game.

Assessing Board Effectiveness

It is rare to find a company that does not conduct a periodic review of the performance of its key personnel. A few years ago, it was similarly rare to find a company that conducted a regular review of the performance of its apex governance body - the board. A few years ago, one could safely say that "while boards often become highly skilled at monitoring and improving the achievement of management, it is far less common for them to give effective consideration to their own performance."[37]

Today, international corporate governance standards and codes increasingly emphasize the need for boards to evaluate their effectiveness. For example, the UK code requires that the board undertake a formal and rigorous annual evaluation of its own performance and its committees and individual directors.[38]

Assessing board performance offers substantial benefits to the company, the board, and the directors individually. According to the King IV Code for Governance Principles in South Africa, "The board should determine its own role, functions, duties and performance criteria as well as that for directors on the board and board committees to serve as a benchmark for the performance appraisal. Yearly assessment should be performed by the chairman or an independent external provider. The results of performance assessment should identify training needs for directors." OECD prescribes that the "Board of listed companies should undergo annual internal assessment covering both the competencies and performance of their members as well as the Board's functioning as a whole."

The ability to look inward is an essential means that directors can identify and correct problems and add real value to the institution. People are often required to possess insight about deficiencies in their intellectual and skills; however, there is a tendency to be blissfully unaware of one's own incompetence.[39]

Regardless of the foregoing, the result of one Harvard study in collaboration with The Miles Group, a consulting and advisory firm, suggests that many board assessments are inadequate. This study, which reviewed 187 boards, discovered "that most board assessments fail to identify and correct poor performance among individual members." As the report goes, only 55 percent of companies that conduct board assessments also carry out individual directors' evaluations, and only 36 percent believe "their company does a very good job of accurately assessing the performance of individual directors."

In the Harvard Business Review (HBR) article titled "What Makes Great Boards Great," Sonnenfeld indicates that the board of directors is the least rigorously examined group of individuals. He lamented this anomaly as he further stated that lack of constructive feedback is self-destructive because people cannot get better without feedback. Accordingly, regardless of how good a board is, it can get better if intelligently evaluated.

In conducting a self-evaluation, directors should review their availability and the use of their time, appropriate use of their skills and experience, knowledge of the company and sector, engagement with other board members, and the dynamics of board operations. A 2017 *HBR* report specifically explained that the more value-producing part of a board evaluation process is to review the contribution of individual directors and the interpersonal and group dynamics among board members. However, this is the more difficult part; thus, this evaluation aspect is not usually performed rigorously, and sometimes it is omitted entirely.

Looking inwards or conducting an evaluation is vital in corporate governance as it helps boards demonstrate progress and chart the way forward. Just as evaluation is essential, it is equally important to evaluate constantly and ensure appropriate competencies still exist. Companies evolve, the external environment changes very quickly, so it is imperative to ensure that boards are sufficiently agile to adapt to changes without losing traction. A thought expressed by Sir Bryan Nicholson, former chairman of the Financial Reporting Council, "[Board] evaluation is essential to improving [a board's] performance—you cannot begin to address your weaknesses unless you know what they are." *An inward look reveals what changes are required!*

One of the challenges with most board assessment tools is that they become oversimplified in trying to be broadly applicable or provide a one-size-fits-all perspective. Every board is different, and board roles, needs, priorities, and capacities vary depending on the company's size, age, stage in its life cycle, and other factors. Thus, a strong board performance may look quite different from one board to the next. It is also important not to stop at assessing performance (what the board does) but to seek out indicators that the board has an equally strong purpose (why the board does what it does) and a set of reliable procedures (how the board does what it does).

There are various approaches for boards to adopt and adapt in assessing their performance. Some options involve simple worksheets or checklists that can be entirely self-administered by the board. Other options involve the use of more sophisticated tools or a facilitated process. A worksheet or checklist-approach type self-assessment focuses on basic board functioning and can be helpful to boards that want to monitor their performance over time or in between more in-depth assessments. A facilitated evaluation typically addresses the critical areas of board responsibility. It often goes deeper into the quality of board interactions and engagement based on the objectivity of an expert evaluator. A facilitated assessment can often lead to more significant board transformation.

Resistance, Rewards, Risks, and Resolutions

Directors sometimes resist the need to assess their performance. One technique for reducing directors' opposition to the assessment process is redefining the objective and refocusing on improving performance rather than criticizing performance or behavior. Treating assessments as a creative process, rather than a critiquing process, may make it more acceptable.

Common reasons why evaluations do not take place include

- Some directors may feel uncomfortable about being evaluated.
- Day-to-day pressures cause the board to delay the evaluation.
- An assessment may be perceived as a sign that the board lacks trust or confidence in the CEO's performance.
- The board feels it lacks the skills and expertise to undertake an effective self-evaluation.
- A dysfunctional board.
- The CEO, chairman, or founder may be dominating the board and be concerned about the issues that an evaluation may raise.
- Previous board assessments were ineffective.

There are many rewards for completing a board assessment properly. These may include, among others,

- Creating an opportunity for board members to self-reflect, critically analyze, and evaluate improvement areas;
- Providing board members with a tool to measure their effectiveness and efficiencies;
- Stimulating a culture of learning and improving the effectiveness and efficiency of the board and board members;
- Improving the working relationship within the board, the company secretarial function, and executive management;
- Identifying action plans to improve the reporting of information for efficient and effective decision-making;
- Improving the working relationship between board committees and the board, including streamlining of the report and eliminating duplication of effort; and
- Identifying the training needs of board members to ensure they are kept abreast of the latest developments.

Board evaluations are inevitably challenging for board members. An improper or poorly crafted board evaluation process may make it difficult for the board to embrace the process. For example, the nature of the questions may leave board members without the opportunity to provide input and feedback on other areas of importance. If internal to the organization, the facilitator may not be independent, and the board maintains the risk of following the facilitator's agenda. The board may wish to raise sensitivities regarding the facilitator (usually, the company secretary); however, it does not have the freedom to do so without creating internal and unnecessary tension. Therefore, board members may be reluctant to embrace the board evaluation when done internally.

While many organizations still prefer an internal board evaluation process, there are direct benefits gained from retaining the services of external, independent evaluators, such as governance advisory firms or external counsel, to mitigate the inherent risks of not completing the evaluation process properly. An independent evaluator provides

- Board members with the platform to speak freely and provide feedback on the company secretariat function without prejudice,
- Reports that maintain the confidentiality and discreetness of information and comments made by board members,
- A formal written report based on themes from consensus views rather than quotes from board members or reporting on isolated instances,
- Experienced individuals to perform interviews of board members,
- Benchmarks of results and draws on previous experiences and knowledge to provide benchmarking of results, and
- Value to the assessment process by assisting with action plans and training programs.

Interestingly, the use of external, independent evaluators to facilitate the board assessment process is increasing. About 27 percent of 2019 Fortune 100 companies disclosed having a third-party facilitate their board assessment at least periodically, typically stated as every two or three years, up from 22 percent in 2018.[40]

Board assessments conducted by third-party experts do yield certain gains. In a publication authored by Elsie Walton for the World Bank Group, this is how one board chairman explained it:

> When people share their thoughts candidly through confidential interviews, we can identify conflict points and tensions in advance and be sure conflicts are surfaced constructively and dealt with effectively. And oftentimes, I prefer this to be done by an objective third party—they will get better information and can deliver feedback as well. I don't need to be the person who's taking sides or

calling someone out—I don't want that legacy in my relationships.[41]
    —*Board Chairman, Fortune 500 Consumer Products*

Observations and Experience with Board Assessment

My experience with board assessment spans over two decades. Although the concept that a board should assess its performance had been accepted for decades, it was not a well-known practice in Nigeria and many other countries in Africa. Board assessment became a requirement in the United Kingdom in 2003 and the United States in 2004.[42] The United Kingdom subsequently updated the code to require that the board report its performance assessment, including how the process was conducted.[43]

It was usually an uncomfortable conversation for boards to agree to assess their practices, particularly by a third party. As the practice of board assessment gained wide international acceptance, sector regulators in Nigeria included the need for board assessment into corporate governance codes. This requirement mandated formal reporting and public disclosure of the outcome of the assessment. This kickstarted a flurry of activities in this area, including an emergent revenue stream for accounting and consulting firms.

Corporate governance advocates affirm that board assessments are instrumental to giving the board a fighting chance to improve itself and its performance. But it does require the chairperson to lead against some likely headwinds. And like so many other solutions to a practical problem, it is only helpful if applied thoughtfully and intelligently.

Over the past three decades, I have conducted and facilitated board assessments with several corporate boards, large and small, young and old, working in different sectors of the economy. I have found that many boards still find it challenging to build the capacity for effective fiduciary governance, in which case, an assessment is often a valuable diagnostic for identifying areas where board education and development are needed.

It would appear that some boards struggle with the realization of their fallibility. Otherwise, there should have been a greater degree of humility in all directors' minds following the series of multitrillion-dollar corporate collapses. All the companies that collapsed, at one point or the other in history, had boards of directors, who, individually, were people of significant stature, wisdom, and judgment. But collectively, they were utterly ineffective.

Most of the boards I worked with have testified that the assessment helped galvanize their thinking about strategic priorities and their role in setting the company's future direction. The assessment process also serves as a springboard for board conversation on how to improve board practices and procedures.

Combining the outcome of the board self-assessment with an objective conversation based on my experience from working with all types of boards helps the board to constructively deal with challenges, see things in new ways, align behind key priorities, and turn action into results.

As stated earlier, continuous improvement is the new mantra for boards and executives. As boards pay attention to the agitations in the business world, they are taking steps to enhance their assessment practices, addressing the need for increased board diversity, expertise, and effectiveness, and better communicating their work to investors and other stakeholders. One director described how an assessment crystallized the board's decision to implement a new practice:

> *"Following a board assessment exercise, we were self-critical about our lack of preparedness for any magnitude of risk beyond the basic. Based on that assessment, the board agreed to regularly review scenarios and assess*

disaster preparedness. And working on the scenarios has really utilized the diverse experience and full knowledge of our directors. Our assessment led us to request that we do a scenario assessment every year, which helped us understand preparedness better and improved our learning and effectiveness overall."

Another challenge I experience is sometimes getting boards to move from board assessments to realistic actions to enhance board effectiveness. There still tends to be a lot of defensiveness and hesitance to take action.

Beyond the Board Assessment

After an evaluation, then what? Directors must take appropriate action based on the result of the evaluation. Actions may involve enhancing diversity on the board by hiring directors with the skills and experience to oversee the risks and opportunities of a transforming industry or providing training for directors in areas where a deficiency is revealed.

What happens after the board assessment report is delivered and the findings are reviewed, discussed, and accepted? Does the board forget about the results of its performance assessment until another assessment? Sadly, this is usually the case. The board's attention moves to other issues, and any momentum for change is lost.

When handled properly, the results of a board assessment process could trigger a range of actions, from relatively minor amendments to board procedures to significant steps toward reviewing the board composition and making changes to board committee structures. Merely outlining the findings of a board assessment does not translate to improvements.

For the exercise to be sufficiently meaningful, the assessment report must result in an actionable plan. Implementing the actions becomes a critical step in the entire assessment process and should deserve the board's full attention. An equally compelling reason for boards to take their performance assessment seriously is that they, like all teams, can benefit immensely from feedback.[44]

Therefore, any agreed actions from an assessment must be implemented and monitored if the board is to improve its performance and effectiveness. Boards can include a review of action steps as an agenda item to be tracked at each meeting. In addition, milestones can be established to achieve the action plans and review progress until all agreed changes are implemented.

Having a road map that captures what is to be done and is being done is another critical step in improving board performance and effectiveness. The road map is an excellent way to see the impact of an assessment from the outset. For example, "quick wins" or "easy fixes" from the process may include a revised agenda or restructured board papers—these can then be crossed off the list of activities.

Longer-term outcomes or more significant changes might require a board paper prepared by a committee, company secretary, or governance champion, recommending a new process or policy to the board for approval. The road map will set out the key steps the board must take to ensure continuous improvement. If this step is neglected, the entire board assessment process will not impact the board's performance.

Here are examples of high-level actions that can be taken following a board assessment:

- Enhanced director orientation programs
- Changes to board structure and composition
- Changes to director tenure or retirement age limits
- Expanded director search and recruitment practices
- Improvements to the format and timing of board materials
- More time to review important matters like strategy and cybersecurity

- Changes to company and board governance documents
- Improved evaluation process

Having skilled and experienced individuals together to form a board will not guarantee that the board is successful. Frequent assessments and making improvements are vital to a successful board. Boards constantly face demands from investors, regulators, stakeholders, and governance experts to assess and explain their performance and composition. Commitment toward a well-managed assessment helps build trust with shareholders and other stakeholders and enables boards to improve performance continuously.

In the words of Brian Tracy, "Continuous learning is the minimum requirement for success in any field." And I would add, continuous practice enhances learning.

Quick Check: Questions for Boards and Executives

- Strategically, self-introspection is a great place to start with every individual, no matter what group you are a member of. Are Board members willing to engage in self-introspection?
- Has the most recent evaluation process enabled the board and individual directors to identify actions to optimize board and director performance and board composition?
- Does the evaluation process provide validation to each director that they are the right director at the right time for the right company?
- Does the board have a common and clear understanding of the term "effectiveness" applied to the board, its committees, and each director?
- Has the board formulated clear goals, objectives, and standards for itself, its committees, and each director that can be referenced during and outside the assessment process?

- Are the standards and requirements that each director must consistently meet to earn renomination clear?
- Does the assessment process include components that occur on a biannual, quarterly, and real-time basis? If not, why not?
- Is the assessment process appropriately synergized with the board's education programs and director-nomination process?

CHAPTER 5

AN OUTWARD LOOK: THE STAKEHOLDER-CENTRIC BOARD

Looking outward collaboratively and becoming stakeholder-centric is the fourth dimension of my proprietary Five-Way-Directional Model©. Looking outward means looking beyond oneself or the company and being mindful of a broad range of stakeholders. International organizations, such as the Organisation for Economic Co-operation and Development (OECD), the United Nations (UN), and the International Labour Organisation (ILO), have all issued guidance regarding appropriate business conduct, sometimes in specific areas.

Sir Adrian Cadbury's description of corporate governance is instructive to initiate the discussion on stakeholders. He said, "Corporate Governance is concerned with balancing economic and social goals and between individual and communal goals. The corporate governance framework is there to encourage the efficient use of resources and equally to require accountability for the stewardship of those resources. The aim is to align as nearly as possible the interests of individuals, corporations, and society."[45]

Good corporate governance is essential to create trust and engagement between companies and their stakeholders, thereby contributing to the companies' long-term success. Stakeholders represent a growing diversity of audiences with different information needs, making for more challenging communications among directors, shareholders, and management.[46]

This chapter presents a structured and practical case for stakeholder engagement as a means to business success and societal trust, which requires the Board's attention as they *look outward*.

Stakeholder engagement is not an attempt to burden the board with additional responsibilities. Instead, effective board leadership involves integrating stakeholder engagement within the board's core responsibilities as part of best practice. Effective stakeholder engagement also helps embed openness and collaboration in a company's overall business approach.

Identifying Your Stakeholders

The term "stakeholder" has been used since at least the 1930s, when a Harvard Law professor, E. Merrick Dodd, officially identified four major groups of business stakeholders: shareowners, employees, customers, and the general public.[47] A 1963 internal memo at the Stanford Research Institute used the term to refer to "those groups without whose support the organization would cease to exist."

Stakeholders, by definition, have a stake in the company and have the possibility of gaining benefits or experiencing losses or harm as a result of the company's business operations. Examples of stakeholders include

- Employees
- Shareowners
- Suppliers
- Customer/Clients and their families
- Regulatory agencies
- Volunteers
- Donors
- Financiers/Investors
- Local and central governments
- General public
- Media
- Local communities
- Nongovernmental organizations

The stakeholders of each company are different depending on the sector, stage of business, and locality. Besides, in large companies, other divisions, departments, or operational entities may have different key stakeholder groups.

To govern effectively, boards must *look outward* and be conscious of the stakeholder environment in which they operate and understand the interests, concerns, and needs of these stakeholders to make informed decisions about balancing the interests of all the groups to which they may have some obligation. Engaging with stakeholders has real governance implications because it goes to the heart of how power and authority are understood and used.

In certain instances, boards may also have obligations under the law about how they work with stakeholders. A company may have legally binding contracts with suppliers or customers. In countries where certain employee rights are protected legally, society has agreed that companies have responsibilities to employees. While companies have legal obligations to investors, most also have legal obligations to other stakeholder groups.[48] At the heart of stakeholder engagement is the acknowledgment that companies are impacted by and have an impact on those with whom they interact.

People, Planet, and Profit

The phrase *people, planet, and profit* used to describe the triple bottom line (TBL), and the goal of sustainability was coined by John Elkington in 1994.[49] The concept of TBL demands that a company's responsibility lies with stakeholders rather than shareholders. According to the stakeholder theory, the business entity should be used as a vehicle for coordinating stakeholder interests instead of solely seeking to maximize shareholder (owner) profit.[50]

In some more detail, the *people, planet, and profit* agenda can be described as follows[51]:

- People: This refers to the positive and negative impact a company has on its most important stakeholders. These include employees, their families, customers, suppliers, communities, and any other person affecting or affected by the company.
- Planet: This refers to the impact a company has on its natural environment. This includes reducing its carbon footprint, using

natural resources, toxic materials, and so on, and the active removal of waste, reforestation, and restoration of natural harm.

- Profit: This reflects a company's economic impact. It is the creation of economic outcomes, such as creating employment, generating innovation, and paying taxes, to ensure that prosperity is realized.

Prado-Lorenzo and Garcia-Sanchez concluded in a study that directors are still basically focused on their traditional responsibility of creating economic value. They believe that contrary to the prescribed outward look, this focus does not promote the accountability process before other stakeholders. They should instead seamlessly incorporate today's broader business world concepts, which include their more comprehensive commitment to society.[52]

More than ever before, following the COVID-19 pandemic, boards and executives have a unique platform and an expectation from growing numbers of stakeholders to shape societal discourse, going beyond traditionally-defined CSR to address societal issues at every stage of their value chain. This is a massive opportunity for companies to help reshape the business ecosystem more inclusively. It is also a serious challenge for them to pursue broader societal objectives in a way that can simultaneously contribute significantly to their commercial success.[53]

This level of engagement is vital to the board's oversight function for two fundamental reasons:

The first is that investors, financiers, shareowners increasingly want companies to adopt a triple-bottom-line approach. There is a growing number of socially conscious investors who see environmental, social, and governance (ESG) issues as an essential criterion for investing, in addition to meeting financial performance goals.

Today, investors are avoiding putting their money into industries that do not align with their values and using their investment positions to push for what they see as positive corporate change with broader societal impact. The 2017 A. T. Kearney Foreign Direct Investment Confidence Index results affirm this trend by revealing the extent to which investors believe business leaders should play an active role in shaping government policy around sustainability/ESG.

The second reason is that many consumers want companies to play an active role in addressing societal issues. An A. T. Kearney survey of four hundred senior executives of the world's leading corporations finds that nearly seven in ten executives believe they will increasingly be expected to play important roles in society beyond meeting the narrow business interest of their companies. This statistic holds true irrespective of region or industry.

The survey findings are consistent with the 2018 Edelman Trust Barometer results, which show that citizens expect business leaders to be proactive about social change. Employees are increasingly turning to the board and executives for guidance on broader social issues.

Besides, the younger generation is increasingly voting with their wallets for values-based, sustainable, engaging, and socially conscious brands. Consequently, brands with active engagement with society and are more strongly associated with these values are more likely to carve out a competitive advantage.

Globally, many countries are going through a process of either reviewing their codes or developing new guidelines for governance to ensure that practices are aligned to the new realities of an ever-changing business and regulatory environment. These revisions are laying credence to the importance of ESG and stakeholder engagement to corporate citizenship. Board members must be aware of these revisions and formulate strategies to adopt and apply new and emerging stakeholder-centric principles.

Businesses may be prodded to *look outward* by external triggers or by national and regional initiatives that governments and NGOs may wage. On the other hand, approaches may be internally prompted by a response to a need, such as a crisis or a problem closer to the company. For example, companies may respond to the health issues in Africa and offer prevention campaigns to support employees' health. Or they may work on preserving natural resources within the tourism industry to generate future eco-tourism business.

The Business Case for Stakeholder Engagement

Companies that excel at stakeholder engagement excel in business. The skills developed through effective stakeholder engagement are invaluable in an increasingly complex world where companies deal with many different relationships that potentially impact their business. For businesses with diverse geographical locations, this can be particularly challenging.

Considering stakeholder concerns and interests can improve relationships with stakeholder groups, making it easier for a company to operate. It may lead to ideas for products or services that will address stakeholder needs and allow the company to reduce costs and increase wealth. More details on the benefits that can accrue to companies when the board *looks outward* and engages with stakeholders[54] are described below:

Value and Wealth Creation: Corporate wealth is the cumulative result of positive corporate performance over time, including all the assets, competencies, and revenue-generating capacities of a company. Successful companies can pay higher salaries, offer better career opportunities, provide more significant customer benefits, respond better to adversity, and provide more value for shareowners. One of the factors in determining corporate wealth is the value of relational assets, including stakeholder linkages and reputation.[55] The failure to establish and maintain productive relationships with stakeholders is a failure to manage a company's capacity to generate wealth effectively.

The table below outlines the sources of a company's wealth attributable to different stakeholder groups. This shows the extent to which effective management of stakeholders by a focused board can enhance value and wealth creation.

Stakeholder Group	Contributions to Value and Wealth
Investors and Lenders	• Capital, equity, and debt • Financial market recognition (reducing borrowing costs and risks)
Employees	• Enhanced productivity based on the development of human capital • Collaborative workplace relations
Unions	• Workforce stability and conflict resolution • An enabling work environment
Customers/Users	• Brand loyalty and reputation • Repeated/Related purchases • Collaborative design, development, and problem-solving • Increased sales and customer retention, evidenced by
Supply Chain	• Enhanced supply chain management resulting in network and value chain efficiencies • Collaborative cost-reducing processes and technologies
Joint Venture Partners and Alliances	• Strategic resources and capabilities that boost corporate sustainability

Local Communities	• Stable business and investment climate • License to operate • Mutual support and accommodation
Governments	• Macroeconomic and social policies • Support business growth and expansion
Regulatory Authorities	• Validation of product/service characteristics or quality levels • Establishment of a level playing field by enacting appropriate rules
SOURCE: Adapted from Post, Preston, and Sachs (2002)[56]	

Figure 1 The sources of company wealth attributable to different stakeholder groups.

Risk Reduction: Businesses can effectively reduce financial, reputational, and political risks by engaging with stakeholders. This may be more applicable to companies with highly visible, prominent brands, which can be more vulnerable to reputational risk. Understanding stakeholders' concerns and interests helps a company manage environmental and social expectations better, resulting in reduced risk of brand assassination, improved access to capital and insurance, cost savings, and reduced vulnerability to regulatory changes.

Opportunities for Innovation: Where there is a risk, there is also opportunity. Stakeholder engagement gives companies a better understanding of the society in which they operate. It can provide a way to better understand how to improve services and products to meet changing consumer needs. It may also be a way to get a different point of view about corporate operations, which could lead to ideas for improvement. In Bangladesh, Prof. Muhammad Yunus's interactions with poor Bangladeshis led him to reconsider some of the basic premises of conventional banking in setting up Grameen Bank. As a result, he invented the concept of microfinance, for which he won the Nobel Peace Prize in 2006.

Without engaging stakeholders in strategic conversations, the board runs the risk of developing a very myopic and limited perspective of the company, its capabilities, and potential. In his book *Why Smart Executives Fail: And What You Can Learn from Their Mistakes*,[57] Sidney Finkelstein, a professor at the Tuck Business School at Dartmouth University describes this mentality as one of the most common triggers for catastrophic leadership failure:

> I will be remiss if I do not sound a word of caution that reactive engagement or engaging with stakeholders only when there is no other alternative in a crisis situation attempts to rebuild a corporate reputation with stakeholders that was never very strong, to begin with. In contrast, proactive and interactive engagement reduces the possibility of a reputational crisis. It builds goodwill and a sense of cooperation with stakeholders that can be an asset in a crisis.[58]

The Board's Role in Stakeholder Engagement

In most jurisdictions, the Companies Act places the onus on directors to balance and prioritize the potentially competing interests of stakeholders to ensure business success. The board's role in embracing its external stakeholders continues to evolve, but its response must be defined within the board's general roles and responsibilities.

While board structures and responsibilities vary according to local norms, laws, and regulations, most boards are responsible for, among other things, shaping the company's framework for accountability, control, and risk management. This is where stakeholder engagement relates to board leadership. The board of directors can play an essential role in ensuring that an *outward-looking* approach, including transparency, integrity, and win-win relationship with stakeholders, is valued within the company and that these values are implemented.

Stakeholder engagement is a critical component of good governance. A company's relationships with its stakeholders can significantly impact its ability to achieve its goals. As such, boards should oversee the process of stakeholder engagement and be satisfied that their stakeholders are identified and understood. An *outward look* adds great value and ensures sustainability.

Boards need to consider how their decisions impact stakeholders. An appreciation of the stakeholders' needs and expectations will increase the chances of their decisions leading to the desired outcome. Understood in this context, considering the influence of stakeholders is an integral part of the risk management process. The board is meant to authorize stakeholder engagement frameworks that help guide a company's work by identifying relevant stakeholders and setting the parameters for engaging with them.

In some circumstances, directors themselves may become actively involved in managing relationships. For example, it is sometimes helpful for the chairperson or other directors to attend meetings with politicians in advocacy settings or meet with significant donors. This can help build personal relationships and reflect the board's commitment to engaging with important stakeholders.

A study conducted in 2019 revealed that stakeholder engagement was the number one risk for boards for the second year in a row.[59] A further analysis was done to identify the key actions that boards that have improved their stakeholder engagement performance year on year have taken to manage this risk. Here is a summary of some of the actions taken by those boards that have enhanced their stakeholder engagement:

- Assessment: These boards *looked outward* and took steps to identify the company's key stakeholders, checking the board's and executive's capabilities for stakeholder engagement and upskilling as necessary.

- Planning: Based on the assessment outcomes, these boards created targeted stakeholder engagement plans that established each stakeholder's level of importance in alignment with the company's strategy, defining specific engagement approaches, responsible persons, reporting structures, and KPIs.

- Training: Board members, CEOs, and executive teams received training on best-practice approaches to stakeholder engagement to ensure a clear understanding of the importance of stakeholder engagement.

- Strategic Influence: Feedback from stakeholders is factored into the company's strategic planning process. Some boards introduced presentations from stakeholder representatives at their strategic planning days, while others invited key stakeholders to participate in the planning sessions. Other boards communicated the company's strategy to stakeholders and invited feedback. Some boards are having key stakeholder groups review and comment on the company's approach to ESG performance.

- Continuous Engagement: There is a range of initiatives from boards to build their capabilities for continuous stakeholder engagement. One board introduced a process of stakeholder mapping exercise for the board, executive team, and senior staff members to better understand their networks and relationships with the company's stakeholders. Another board introduced quarterly "letters from the chair" to critical stakeholders and extended invitations to corporate events.

- Measurement and Evaluation: Some boards introduced new metrics (that go beyond the number of visits or meetings) for measuring the effectiveness of their stakeholder engagement efforts. These include measuring the health of the relationships with stakeholders through expert third-party reviews, interviews, and feedback, providing insight into stakeholders' perspectives, and building trust. It also gives the board some early warning signs of relationships that might not be as good as initially believed or expected.

An example of how a board is in the loop of stakeholder engagement is captured by the pragmatic story of *XYZ Ltd.*

XYZ Ltd. developed a comprehensive stakeholder engagement framework that identified who their stakeholders are and how the company understood their needs and expectations. The framework sets out a principles-based approach to stakeholder engagement grounded in respect, participation, and transparency.

As part of their formal decision-making process, the board considered how their decisions would impact and may be impacted by stakeholders. To maintain an ongoing connection with stakeholders, board meetings begin with a "client story," which helps directors focus their minds on how their work impacts stakeholders. Directors also regularly engaged with stakeholders through site visits and participating in the town hall and consultative forums.

XYZ Ltd. actively sought opportunities to gather feedback from stakeholders and used mechanisms such as client surveys and market research to develop a more holistic picture of performance. They have also established policies for responding to compliments and complaints so that feedback is appropriately acted on.

Because stakeholder engagement is critical, board members should be briefed about engagement practices and outcomes. Just as the board should be involved in financial reporting, it should also oversee nonfinancial reporting, including the stakeholder engagement process. In some companies, such reporting is governed by the audit committee.

There are also boards with committees dedicated to corporate responsibility or sustainability that monitor or oversee stakeholder engagement and sustainability reporting.

In most instances, stakeholders are not represented on company boards. An advisory body can provide representation for stakeholders through a second tier within the governance structure.[60] This can take the form of an independent advisory committee or stakeholder panel to serve as a proxy for stakeholder groups. Having a non-executive director involved in or as chair of the group can further ensure that recommendations are shared with the board, allowing the board to take a direct interest in these issues and how they might inform critical decisions. Notably, the advisory committee should be given direct access to the board to ensure that the board gets a broad sense of outside perspectives of the company.

Reputation and Sustainability Will Feature in the Future

About twenty years ago, while at PwC, I invested time and resources in building a reputation-assurance service. Needless to say, it did not gain much internal support nor traction with clients, perhaps because I was not adept at communicating the importance of the matter or because the market was not ready for such a service at the time—or both. Also, I found one of the presentations used in my archives titled "Managing Reputational Risks, Creating Sustainable Shareholder Value," dated October 19, 2001. While writing this section, I reminisced about it. How time flies and the issues have remained the same with increasing relevance.

At that time, I closely followed the writings and works of Dr. Charles Fombrun, founder and chairman of Reputation Institute and former professor of management at the Stern School of Business, New York. And as I conclude this chapter, two of his quotes come readily to mind: The first one is "A company's reputation is rooted in the perception of its employees, customers, investors, and other stakeholders. Therefore, reputational capital is among the most important success drivers of the company." The second quote is, "Effective reputation risk management helps an organization *build competitive advantage by turning stakeholders into advocates.*" These quotes, which were apt twenty years ago, are still relevant today and align with the findings of many recent studies.

Today there has been a significant shift in focus as boards concentrate on areas that take the long-term view. In a 2020 Heidrick & Struggles survey on the board of the future, the researchers asked directors which areas boards lead today and which areas they are likely to lead in five years. This question was to enable an understanding of the emerging trends on board agendas. According to respondents, creating long-term value climbs 25 percentage points on the board's agenda in five years compared with current levels.

Respondents also expect significant increases in the board's role regarding corporate reputation, embedding a purpose-driven culture within the company (inward look), and horizon scanning and scenario planning (forward look). Traditionally, the CEO and the executive team have mainly driven several of these responsibilities, with boards having relatively distant and infrequent oversight.

The importance of the need for the board to take an outward look cannot be overemphasized. Corporate reputation offers a good reason why boards feel they must now take an active role in such areas. In this age of the rise of social media, a negative story, whether true or not, can severely damage a company's standing within a matter of days. As Warren Buffett, chairman, and CEO of Berkshire Hathaway, said many years ago, *it takes twenty years to build a reputation and five minutes to ruin it.*

Reputation and sustainability are two sides of a coin. For many companies, sustainability is an increasingly important element of purpose and a reputational factor.[61] Sustainability issues and, consequently, reputation are taking on greater importance for consumers and investors alike. Thus, board members feel a growing responsibility to ensure that they think not only about areas where boards have long had clear accountability or oversight, such as compensation, but also more broadly about factors that can affect reputation.

Boards already have oversight over environmental, social, and governance (ESG) assessments. These issues have become more important to customers, employees, and other stakeholders and influence innovation, operations, procurement, and even corporate travel. There is a clear need for boards to ensure the management team takes a comprehensive and proactive view of these issues. "The rise of ESG on the corporate agenda has been a major development, and expectations from companies are only going to increase," says Ian Bull, interim non-executive chairman and non-executive director for FTSE 250 companies.

Many respondents to the Heidrick & Struggles survey described what they wanted their board's legacy to be from a long-term, sustainable perspective, such as "a sustainable and successful business in the eyes of employees, customers, and shareholders," "value creation for various company shareholders," and "a socially responsible and sustainable business model."

Those responses are similar to the results of another study conducted by Odgers Berndtson Ireland, in partnership with The Governance Company. The Odgers Berndtson survey asked directors what they considered the most crucial competencies, behaviors, and soft skills for future directors to ensure boardroom effectiveness.[62] The issue of sustainability and its potential impact on reputation emerged. Therefore, directors must embrace environmental, social, and governance factors, which many investors use to measure a business's sustainability and reputation.

In a white paper released in 2018, the World Economic Forum defined agile governance as "adaptive, human-centered, inclusive and sustainable policymaking, which acknowledges that policy development is an increasingly multi-stakeholder effort." The Five-Way-Directional Model© provides a framework for directors to address multiple stakeholder concerns and find appropriate ways to engage effectively. Tracking and reporting engagement with stakeholders will be helpful to demonstrate proactive actions as boards navigate future business issues.

Quick Check: Questions for Boards and Executives

- Has the board been evaluated for stakeholder engagement skills and experience?
- Has the board completed a stakeholder engagement training?
- Who are the company's stakeholders, and how are the needs of stakeholders considered by the board?
- How do stakeholders perceive the company, and what is the impact of this?
- How does the board access and respond to feedback from stakeholders?
- Is there a priority map for who is and is not a key stakeholder? Have their unique requirements for engagement been identified?
- Does key stakeholder feedback form an input to the corporate strategic planning process?
- Does a key stakeholder engagement/communication plan reviewed and approved by the board exist? Is it reviewed periodically?
- Are the outcome measures for your stakeholder engagement (not just numbers of visits or meetings) clearly defined?
- Is the health of the relationships with key stakeholders being measured and reported to the board?
- Is your board addressing all the stakeholders, not just the shareholders? If so, how, and what's the order of priority?
- How well is your board cultivating a deeper understanding of the community or communities it serves and bringing

stakeholders' perspectives, needs, feedback, and priorities into the strategic boardroom discussions?

- Is the board ever at risk of making decisions without fully understanding how these decisions may affect the stakeholders?

CHAPTER 6

AN UPWARD LOOK: A PERSONAL REFLECTION

The final dimension of the Five-Way-Directional Model© is the upward look. This dimension delves into the personal arena of individual board members. As I wrote this chapter, I asked my eldest daughter, who happened to be in the room, what comes to mind when she sees someone looking upward. She responded that when people look upward, they are probably thinking deeply (reflection) and searching for answers (exploring). Looking up often depicts giving up on ineffective "self-reliant" efforts and seeking support from a superior power (above).

In executing their role on the board, each director contributes their opinions or perspectives based on their values, ethics, skill set, attitudes, mindset, fears, faith, etc. Ultimately, the output from the boardroom is the combination of the perspectives of individual directors and, over time, collectively evolve into the group dynamics and board culture. Investors believe that good governance begins with a great board of directors. However, they also understand that each director must be independent, ethical, committed, capable, and appropriately experienced[63] for a board to be considered good and effective.

Moral Intelligence in the Boardroom

I agree with John Maxwell, who said in his book *Ethics 101* that ethics is a personal issue.

Ethics, morals, and core values are fundamental phenomena in business, even though most people do not pay much attention to these terms. The terms are used interchangeably and together, and they guide people in their decisions. Following the cases of corporate scandals and collapses, it is clear that the deterioration of ethics and core values in governance contributed to those failures and continues to do the same today.

Many boards ensure that the company develops and promotes its core values, ethical and responsible decision-making, and complies with best governance practices. A company's core values and ethical guidelines typically address code of conduct, conflicts of interest, confidentiality, fair dealing, protection of and use of the company's assets, compliance with laws and regulations, and encourages the reporting of unlawful/unethical behavior.

Consequently, directors should also act ethically; hence, the subject of moral intelligence (MQ) is relevant in a book for boards. Moral intelligence is newer and less studied than the more established cognitive, emotional, and social intelligence but has excellent potential to improve our understanding of expected leadership behavior.[64] Moral intelligence, developed to its fullest by Doug Lennick and Fred Kiel in their book of the same name, has more to do with values and behaviors than what we would think of as "intelligence" or some basic concept of mental acumen such as IQ.[65]

- MQ is the ability to differentiate right from wrong as defined by universal principles.
- MQ is a compass for boards and executives in our modern global business environment.[66]
- MQ is our mental capacity to determine how universal human principles should be applied to our personal values, goals, and actions.[67]
- MQ is the willingness and ability to put something else than oneself at the center of one's reflections[68], and studies show that it is highly associated with leadership effectiveness.
- MQ is the capacity to have strong ethical convictions and act on them.[69] It is a developmental type of reasoning, which suggests that MQ is developed and refined through experience.

The construct of moral intelligence consists of integrity, responsibility, forgiveness, and compassion.[70] These are all key attributes that make for effective leadership and directorship. And since our morals and personal values should be tied to our faith, it makes the call for an upward look critical.

1. *Integrity* creates harmony between what we believe and how we act, doing what we know is right.[71] Elements of integrity are (a) acting consistently with principles, values, and beliefs; (b) telling the truth; (c) standing up for what is right; and (d) keeping promises.[72] Integrity, it has been said, is what a person has when no one is watching.

2. *Responsibility* is the combination of two words, "response" and "ability," and it has these three competencies, which are (a) being responsive and taking personal responsibility, (b) admitting mistakes and failures, and (c) embracing responsibility for serving others.

3. *Forgiveness* is a fundamental leadership principle because, without tolerance for mistakes and acknowledgment of human imperfection, we are likely to be rigid and inflexible, thereby reducing the common good. Forgiveness involves (a) letting go of one's own mistakes and (b) letting go of others' mistakes.

4. *Compassion* is actively caring about others, which shows our respect for them.

Lennick and Kiel demonstrate that top-performing companies have directors and executives who promote moral intelligence throughout their organizations "because they believe it's the right thing to do. They [also] produce consistently high performance almost any way you can measure it—gross sales, profits, talent retention, company reputation, and customer satisfaction."[73] They are scrupulous in their efforts to use morally justifiable means to pursue their moral goals. And they demonstrate humility and willingness to risk their own self-interest for the sake of their moral goals.[74]

Moral intelligence could also include setting goals, recognizing problems, deciding on the right thing to do, acting appropriately, and persevering. Studies show that moral intelligence is highly associated with leadership effectiveness. Therefore, a director with high moral intelligence will be more effective on the board. Boards with directors whose moral intelligence is high will perform well.

Each director faces a series of "moral moments," personal choice points, that require a clear decision in boardroom interactions. A director might find themselves in moral dilemmas at these points, so taking an upward look and connecting to one's faith often helps make these moral moments easier to navigate.

According to Dwight D. Eisenhower, "To be a leader, a man must have followers. And to have followers, a man must have their trust and confidence. Hence, the supreme quality for a leader is unquestionably integrity. Without it, no real success is possible, whether on a section gang, a football field, in an army, or an office. If a man's associates find him guilty of being phony, if they find that he lacks forthright integrity, he will fail. His teachings and actions must square with each other. The first great need, therefore, is integrity and high purpose."[75]

Moral intelligence in the boardroom should be in high demand.

Stewardship in the Boardroom

The financial crisis of 2008-2009 led to legal or bankruptcy issues for several large and well-known financial institutions worldwide.[76] Cases of fraud, accounting scandals, and business failures were the trigger for the global crisis.[77] Analyzing these corporate failures, regulators tagged the lack of professional competencies and integrity of board members as one reason that led to bankruptcies.[78] Other commentators pointed to a lack of stewardship and commitment as the leading cause of the crisis. They believe that most directors were assessed as competent (experienced, skilled, intelligent, etc.) before being considered for board appointments. These attributes did not preclude them from the crisis because they lacked a sense of stewardship.

Reading the book *From Third World to First: The Singapore Story: 1965-2000* by Lee Kuan Yew, I reflected on a few leadership lessons that support the importance of a personal drive toward sound stewardship and how this can make a director very effective. Being focused on being a good steward earns on the trust of key stakeholders:

1. Lee Kuan Yew demonstrated a commitment to the cause to serve Singaporeans. This earned him and his team the trust of the people. He attested to this himself: "Our greatest asset was

the trust and confidence of the people."[79] As a director, one must assure themselves that they can earn the trust of shareholders, other directors, and stakeholders. Your greatest asset is that these constituencies trust that you are committed to serving them. That element of trust and confidence defines your credibility in the marketplace. You must ensure that your credibility is intact before, during, and after every board interaction.

2. He believed in winning the trust and confidence of the people by sheer dint of hard work. He shared that he and his team earned the trust and confidence of the people by the fight they had to put up on behalf of the people. Similarly, directorship comes with significant responsibilities, and there will be a series of battles to put up with not to compromise your values and deliver on your commitment.

3. Once trust is gained, it is vital to safeguard it. Lee Kuan Yew said they were "careful not to squander this newly gained trust" by misgovernance and corrupt practices. "We had to fight every inch of the way to establish continued confidence in our integrity, competence, and judgment."[80] One can draw a parallel between this and the fact that every director who considers themselves trusted by peers and stakeholders must ensure that the status remains.

4. "The task of the leaders must be to provide or create a strong framework within which they can learn, work hard, be productive, and be rewarded accordingly. And this is not easy to achieve." Vision, structure, and determination are paramount to effective board leadership. Lee Kuan Yew was a brilliant, clear-eyed, far-sighted statesman, and he was determined to serve. Singapore's political stability, rapid economic growth, and rising affluence between 1959 and 1990 were not accidental but the result of his dynamic leadership and focused stewardship.

5. Leadership often entails tough, unpopular decisions. In the Singaporean case, Lee Kuan Yew was not afraid of being out of favor. He said, "I have never been overconcerned or obsessed with opinion polls or popularity polls. I think a leader who is, is

a weak leader."[81] Over the years, I have discovered that unusual and (sometimes) unpopular ideas and perspectives come from a director who is independent of a subject matter or an initiative. Perhaps because the person can see and assess without being biased or affected by the norms and traditions associated with the decision and is not opposed to conflicting ideas. Some directors avoid conflict by not voicing a divergent view. Having the courage to share an unusual idea or make an unpopular decision is a virtue to be embraced. Sharing a perspective from a place of relative weakness or disadvantage requires courage, and your stewardship depends on it.

I read a fascinating account that captures the essence of stewardship:

A rider on horseback, many years ago, came upon a squad of soldiers who were trying to move a heavy piece of timber. A corporal stood by, giving lordly orders to "heave." But the piece of timber was a trifle too heavy for the squad.

"Why don't you help them?" asked the quiet man on the horse, addressing the important corporal.

"Me? Why, I'm a corporal, sir!" Dismounting, the stranger carefully took his place with the soldiers.

"Now, all together boys, heave!" he said. And the big piece of timber slid into place. The stranger mounted his horse and addressed the corporal.

"The next time you have a piece of timber for your men to handle, Corporal, send for the commander in chief."

The horseman was George Washington, the first American president.

George Washington was a great example of a leader who was a great soldier and servant to those he led. Little wonder he pioneered a new nation.

Being Inspired and Inspiring

During the COVID-19 pandemic, the importance of finding inspiration and being inspiring became more evident to me. This epiphany happened during a webinar in which I heard a CEO describe how she needed to be inspired to inspire her employees. She also shared how some directors on the company's board were "energizers" because they stayed positive, were hopeful, and inspiring. On the converse, some directors could be described as "energy drainers."

According to her analogies, "inspiration" is like energy, and one can intentionally find inspiration. In her case, she tended to lean more toward relating to or discussing issues with the "energizing" directors, particularly when it is not a matter to be addressed by the entire board. During the COVID-19 crisis, I listened to a leadership podcast, which mentioned that those who have faith could cope better in a crisis. These leaders seem to be infused with divine inspiration. A realization that there is a superior and sovereign being, God, and a greater purpose gives new perspectives and a lot of inspiration.

Inspirational leadership inspires action, significantly raises individual and team performance levels, and ignites creativity and audacious innovation. It truly unlocks latent potential by tapping into the inner motivation and values and inspiring people to follow their passion and move toward ambitious goals. One of my favorite leadership descriptions is that by John Quincy Adams, the sixth president of the United States. He said, "If your actions inspire others to dream more, learn more, do more, and become more, you are a leader."

A board, through its directors, provides leadership to the company to achieve its purpose, which includes inspiring the executive teams to exceed their potential, particularly during a crisis. The executive team, in turn, inspires the employees to achieve corporate goals. Any time is a good time to be an inspiring leader, but you cannot be inspiring if you are uninspired. As a leader, you cannot afford to be frazzled because people look up to you. It would help if you had *someone* to look upward to.

The business world needs inspired and inspirational boards and executives. However, being inspired is an art, and building one's inspirational capacity is a deliberate act. Looking upward enables a board member to embark on self-reflection and discovery, which are essential in developing their own personal style.

Work First versus Family First

Work-life balance has recently taken the attention of researchers and executives. According to Wikipedia, *work-life balance* is the equilibrium between personal (family) life and career work. Lillian Moller Gilbreth established the philosophical basis for work-life balance.

In the rapidly-changing work environment, time pressures seem ever-increasing, and new digital tools allow work and board meetings to be conducted anytime and anywhere. These are just two factors that make it more and more difficult for directors to integrate work and family life. Consequently, there is a need for flexible and innovative solutions to manage the work-family interface.

Often directors (some of whom are over-boarded already) seek to give 100 percent to work life and family life and never really succeed. Inevitably, something suffers, and often it is their family (spouse, children, parents, siblings, etc.). The family gets sidelined in favor of seemingly urgent official or business needs. Arguably, this is more of a concern for younger board members and executives who have young families. Nonetheless, those in their twilight years who have spent most of their lives disengaged from their families can relate to it and may regret it too.

There are two perspectives of work-life balance discourse:

Conventional wisdom suggests that the work-versus-family tension is caused by business realities that are simply beyond our control. Consider the nature of board membership and executive-level commitments. Some require travel, and there is often no way around it, although the COVID-19 travel restrictions have unearthed other options. Many require long hours to meet deadlines and pressuring projects. And in an increasingly competitive environment, one is often compelled to stay late at work, regardless of one's personal situation.

Our culture has now evolved to a point where professional success demands more personal commitment and flexibility on our part than ever before. The culprit, we reason, is the unalterable nature of business. Occasionally, this has some merit, but the casualty is the family.

Unconventional wisdom (the Bible's perspective) suggests that the work-family dilemma may often be a function of things internal to ourselves than external situations beyond our control. It does not point to others, such as an urgent board appointment, board committee deadlines, or a demanding chairperson, but our ambition, our pride, and in some cases, our greed.

According to unconventional wisdom, each individual needs to be introspective, regularly and candidly scrutinizing why they take on many board appointments or executive responsibilities. Is the reason something elemental like financial security, or are there some nefarious motivators underlying it? Is the reason simply the need to put food on the table and save for the children's tertiary education, or is it more the pursuit of luxuries, a title, prestige, and power? It is essential to distinguish between "legitimate" and "illegitimate" reasons for working so hard and so long. Notice that this is a very personal issue. The tension that some people experience has little to do with the nature of business; instead, the nature of man is the primary culprit.

Aligning personal priorities pays personal and professional dividends. From a strictly financial perspective, a family-sensitive director or executive serves not only the employees' needs but can also meet long-term organizational objectives better than the traditional work-first-oriented leader. The increasing corporate initiatives in this area powerfully testify to this truth.

As much as we would like to think that these trends are a function of a more enlightened, more ethical, and even more compassionate boardroom, much of the movement has a profit motive. A family-friendly work environment can be and is good for business. This notion is becoming so well accepted that periodicals, such as *Business Week* and *Fortune*, which target traditional profit-oriented leaders, are galvanizing action for the family-first concept.

It takes a board member who has a family-sensitive outlook and understands the implications to the company to embrace the concept and support such policies personally. Therefore, the director, who personally understands and appreciates the importance of family, is an asset to the board. They are more likely to find personal fulfillment and can support the cause of employees, thereby promoting commitment, productivity, and long-term retention. Putting family first ahead of work requires humility and faith.

Directors Are on Edge

According to *Cambridge Learner's Dictionary*, "being on edge" is a state of being constantly nervous or worried. A traumatic experience or perceived danger usually causes this. This term provides an excellent graphical description of the disposition of most board members today. Psychological medicine explains that one of the symptoms of "feeling on edge" is constantly being on guard or hypervigilant.

If you are a director in 2021, the chances are that you have had a reasonably recent "traumatic experience" with the COVID-19 pandemic. You will understand that the business landscape is still convulsing, and future problems are imminent if you are perceptive. If you are a director in a future board, you may have just emerged from a crisis, are in the throes of a crisis, or are about to get into one.

The COVID-19 crisis was not just a health crisis but also multidimensional, affecting the economic, business, and political landscapes. It resulted in a massive loss of economic output and financial wealth, psychological consequences, and extended unemployment. Other outcomes include a significant increase in government and regulatory intervention on businesses and the associated costs of implementation. This description of the business environment is sufficient to cause edginess.

Juliet Bourke, the author of the 2016 Australian Institute of Company Directors' bestseller *Which Two Heads Are Better Than One?*, said, "Boards are under extreme pressure to make smart decisions about increasingly complex issues under the spotlight of public scrutiny. Instead of feeling overwhelmed . . . boards can lift their collective intelligence and, therefore, be more confident about their decisions."[82] It is the collective psyche of individual directors who form the boardroom culture and performance. When individual directors do well, the board does well.

On the positive side, though, being on edge prompts action. For example, since a significant proportion of blame is usually attributed to the lack of effectiveness by directors, the onus is on directors to figure out how they might perform differently. Therefore, directors need to know how to deal with the resultant feeling of being on edge without compromising the effective discharge of duties.

My Five-Way-Directional Model© provides a platform for deep self-reflection. This is the last dimension of the model, focusing on self-reflection with a posture of looking upward. Therefore, I will describe how the other four dimensions of this model can be understood, articulated, and harnessed to help individual directors focus their attention to ease the feeling of being on edge.

A forward look: A key area of focus for the future board is looking out for what lies ahead. To effectively govern an institution, directors must pay attention to strategy. The forward-looking board should be composed of directors who are well versed in the complexities of the company, its industry, and relevant laws to provide appropriate input to the strategic plan, which means that each director must also maintain a personal forward look. Enlightened self-interest dictates that a director of the future board should position themselves to add strategic value. *A forward look is vital in this age.*

A backward look: For a director keen to ease the feeling of being on edge, it would be necessary to take a backward look to take stock consciously. Understanding how corporate governance failures contributed to previous corporate scandals and areas where the company's board may have floundered in the past will form the foundation of learning. Many articles and books have been written on the causes of corporate failures that an individual can leverage to learn from past mistakes. The past is a place of reference, not a place of residence. *A backward look is almost always helpful.*

An inward look: As described in chapter 4, an inward look is a synonym for self-examination. There is a need for directors to assess their skills and ensure continued relevance constantly. The outcome of this assessment will help them to determine what course of action to take to upgrade. In addition, a progressive director will be an advocate for periodic board assessments. Looking inward is a critical means by which directors can identify and correct problems and add real value to the company. People are often required to possess insight about deficiencies in their intellectual and skills; however, there is a tendency to be blissfully unaware of one's incompetence.[83] *An inward look reveals what changes are required.*

An outward look: Good corporate governance is essential to create trust and engagement between the directors and executives of a company and their stakeholders, thereby contributing to the business's long-term success. Interaction and communications between directors and stakeholders can be challenging as the stakeholders are increasingly diverse with different information needs. A director can provide leadership for social projects to position their board in a stable and sustainable platform. *An outward look adds excellent value and ensures sustainability.*

An upward look: Overall, the fifth dimension of the model encourages directors to *look upward* and ensure that their responsibilities are delivered with honesty and integrity of purpose. This has been a bold attempt to find new ways to look at directors' challenges and find meaningful and helpful governance solutions.

Quick Check: Questions for Boards and Executives

- What are your ethics and personal values?
- What is your moral intelligence quotient? What is the moral intelligence quotient of the board?
- Have you done your due diligence on the company to ensure you share the same values because good corporate governance must not be compromised?
- Whenever someone mentions your name, does the word "servant" come to their mind?
- Who and what are your sources of inspiration?
- Would you describe yourself as a servant leader? How many of your fellow board members would you describe as such?
- Does your work (stress) affect your family?
- What are the causes and effects of conflict between home and work?

CHAPTER 7

BOARDS' OVERSIGHT OF CRISES

A crisis is a negative deviation from normalcy that is severe and can threaten the existence of a company. It can also be described as an extraordinary event substantially disrupting its operations, business, or reputation. A crisis is, typically, a low-probability, high-impact event that threatens the viability of the organization.

Various factors can cause crises; some are internal to the company, which often relate to weak corporate governance systems. Others are external, outside the company's control, such as the 2020 global COVID-19 pandemic and its attendant problems. There are also situations where internal factors make the company more vulnerable to external factors. All these factors have different effects on the company and may require different responses. Regardless of the cause or causes, a crisis requires immediate and appropriate action by the board and executives to

- contain the impact,
- recover from the shock, and
- minimize the damage to the business.

The COVID-19 pandemic was a crisis that threw many companies a curveball; it was unexpected, threatening, extraordinary, and disruptive. Indeed, the outbreak had the hallmarks of a "landscape-scale" crisis: an unexpected event or sequence of events of enormous scale and overwhelming speed, resulting in a high degree of uncertainty that gives rise to disorientation, a feeling of lost control, and intense emotional disturbance.[84] Some labeled it a black swan event.

My article "Directors in the Age of Being on Edge," in which the Five-Way Directional Model was first articulated, was written as a crisis response. At that time, the only reference point to a crisis was the 2008-09 financial crisis. The article chronicled the root cause of anxiety in many boardrooms as directors grappled with the aftermaths of the financial crisis.

Today, as the world deals with a global public health crisis and its severe economic fallout, only 37 percent of directors said their board fully understands their company's crisis management plan. While boards may give executives thumbs-up for their pandemic response, directors need to ensure that a positive outlook is not masking potential blind spots. Boards should take the time to revisit crisis plans and revise considering what worked and what didn't.[85]

Over the years, some board crises that I have helped my clients to wade through include

- the sudden termination or resignation of a CEO
- a financial crisis caused by a sudden change in the industry
- a significant regulatory action against the company
- a scandal that threatened the company's market status and reputation
- scandals due to mismanagement and fraud
- an unexpected attempt to take over the company
- merger and acquisition that went wrong

When situations like these arise, the board needs to provide high-level strategic oversight of the company's viability, operational resilience, financial well-being, and reputation. Furthermore, the board is required to guide the executive in minimizing the impact and adequately getting prepared.

As boards expect, experience, or engage with crisis, they need to apply the entire Five-Way Directional Model.

1. Look forward - It is vital to look forward and prepare for the future during a crisis. The ability to envision the post-crisis business can strengthen the resilience of the board and executives.
2. Look backward – A backward look is a foundation to learning. Boards should reflect on the past and learn from what went wrong. In crisis preparedness, boards are advised not to underestimate the value of looking back.
3. Look inward – An inward look reveals what changes are required within the corporate architecture to enable the board and executives to stay afloat, survive the crisis, and thrive after that.
4. Look outward – This helps boards and executives understand how stakeholders' needs can be better served during the crisis

and beyond. An outward look adds significant value and ensures business sustainability.

5. Look upward – A crisis is as good a time as any to look upward, soberly yet hopefully, and ensure board and executive responsibilities are delivered with honesty and integrity, aligned with the greater purpose.

The rest of this chapter presents ideas that will help boards and executives improve their practices, enhance their crisis preparedness, recover from the crises, and emerge as more sustainable and competitive businesses.

Typical Corporate Governance Crises

Many corporate crises have their source in the weakness or lack of corporate governance systems. There are four common types of situations/tensions that create corporate-governance-related crises[86]:

1. *Shareholders versus shareholders:* This occurs when majority shareholders make decisions that are good for the short-term profits of some majority investors but not for the long-term interest of the company and of its minority (and often less active) shareholders.
2. *Shareholders versus management*: This happens when shareholders want higher dividend payouts while executives invest more in business operations to yield future profits.
3. *Board versus management*: This occurs when there is a degree of acrimony between the board and management. The board may have lost confidence in the executive team but may not be able to do anything about it, either because there is no succession plan/process or not having appropriate "authority."
4. *Director versus director*: This happens when there is personal animosity, different interests, or hidden agendas (generally because of a lack of leadership by the chairperson to suppress

such behaviors) that lead to a dysfunctional board that cannot make appropriate decisions.

These types of conflicts cause most corporate governance crises. It is essential to note that a conflict is not necessarily a crisis if it is appropriately addressed. Dissents are acceptable if they are constructive and adequately resolved. Therefore, the board must pay attention to warning signals so that conflicts do not degenerate into a crisis. The board must also respond early to warning signals, observe potential trouble spots, and take their oversight responsibilities seriously.

Studies show that three typical barriers prevent boards and executives from taking appropriate actions when necessary to deal with an emerging corporate governance crisis; these are:

1. *Corporate-Political Barriers*
   Influential individuals may have undue political influence on the corporate decision-making process, which impedes rational thinking, such as key decision-makers conflict of interest. There is no easy solution to overcoming corporate-political barriers since changes need to be institution-wide. Therefore, there must be courage and the willingness to make corporate changes for this barrier to be dealt with sustainably at the board level. Having appropriate policies helps provide a guide and safety net for the board.

2. *Organizational Barriers*
   These are typically present in large or diversified companies because of inherent complexity and consequent opacity. For example, interdependencies between departments are ignored, and they operate as "silos," governance becomes fragmented, exposing the company to the risk of inefficiencies.

   In this case, the board needs to establish sound structures and processes of accountability, assign clear responsibilities, and create a high level of transparency. Everyone in the company has a part to play in preventing and dealing with crises; however, they can only play that part if they know it.

3. *Psychological Barriers*

Human beings do not like negative news. There is an inherent tendency to look for good news (for oneself) and information that confirms one's worldview (e.g., to support decisions already taken). Everything else is easily overlooked, hoping that the adverse facts will disappear (though they usually do not).

A diverse board with members who can bring different perspectives to a discussion helps overcome psychological barriers. The board chairperson must maintain an atmosphere that allows for robust debate, ensuring that everyone is entitled to speak up, no one gets offended. The time allocations on the agenda must reflect the business needs and priorities.

The board's ability to overcome these barriers will determine its performance in managing potential corporate governance crises.

Doing Business in a VUCA World

Pearl Zhu, in the book *Digitizing Boardroom: The Multifaceted Aspects of Digital Ready Boards*, rightly said that "in a world of well-defined problems, directors are required to exercise influence over **v**olatility, manage **u**ncertainty, simplify **c**omplexity, and resolve **a**mbiguity in the 21st-century digital environment.[87]

The term VUCA was first used in 1987 by the U.S. Army War College, contributing to American global military strategy. They needed the best way to train a new generation of military leaders to succeed in an unpredictable multilateral world that emerged at the end of the Cold War, which was more complicated than they had faced during the Cold

War. Facilitators at the Army War College described this new context using four words: volatile, uncertain, complex, and ambiguous; and in true military style, this was expeditiously reduced to the acronym VUCA. The business and academic communities have gradually embraced VUCA as a valuable way to describe crises.

A VUCA world describes the state of crisis resulting from political, social, commercial, and technological factors, creating volatility, uncertainty, complexity, and ambiguity. For example, today, talent is more mobile than ever, and the idea of "a job for life" has been replaced by a short-term talent for hire. This trend was exacerbated following the COVID-19 pandemic as talent became highly fluid. In the digital space, technology is moving so fast now that businesses must plan across twelve months horizon (or less) rather than the five-to-ten-year cycles previously adopted. More so, most businesses' entrance into the digital space was very chaotic during the pandemic, providing little or no room for planning, preparation, and postulations.

VUCA accurately describes the global businesses' and economic environments' response to a conflagration of changes. Each word in the VUCA acronym is characteristic of a typical crisis climate.

- *Volatility* refers to the nature and speed of change in the market, industry, or world in general. It is often associated with turbulence (relatively unstable changes). Information is available, and the situation is understandable, but change is frequent and often unpredictable. The business cycle or specific industries' cycles might become more volatile, driven by dramatic changes in currencies or sources of raw materials or by political crises that spill into the business world. This will accelerate the need to adjust to new circumstances even more rapidly and with no stabilizing trend in view to anchor expectations and perspectives.[88] An example would be commodity pricing, which is often quite volatile; crude oil costs have also been volatile.

- *Uncertainty* describes a lack of predictability. Since the emergence of COVID-19, the world as we know it has become less predictable in many ways. There is no assurance about whether an event will have significant ramifications or create substantial change. There is no consensus or even a dominant trend that can be followed. Rather, there are contradicting developments appearing simultaneously (e.g., inflation with sluggish demand, low-interest rates, and low investments) or at different times in different regions. A case in point is antiterrorism initiatives, which are generally plagued with uncertainty; many causes of terrorism are commonly understood but not exactly when and how they could spur attacks.[89]

- Complexity indicates the number and variety of issues at play, many interconnected elements forming an elaborate network of information and procedures. So there is a high degree of interconnectedness between the various factors, which create confusion and make any form of rational analysis challenging. This network of information and procedures is often multiform and convoluted. For example, business in new countries usually involves navigating a complex web of tariffs, laws, regulations, and logistics issues. Regulatory and political interventions might become more frequent and impact not only one specific country but also the supply chains, trade relations, and business model of a globally operating industry.

- Ambiguity depicts the vagueness of reality. It is like walking through a fog. It projects a situation where there is little or no information to make logical decisions. Causal relationships are unclear as there are no antecedents or precedents. We describe this as unprecedented times. For instance, the COVID-19 pandemic forced many companies to leap into the digital world, which was ambiguous for some. Companies are still learning how customers will access and experience business information and engagement given new technologies.

In the thick of the pandemic and necessitated lockdowns, a friend said to me that she wonders how the pandemic will play out and what the new normal will be. My response was "No one knows." And that is what we know for sure because we were experiencing uncontrolled (and uncontrollable) changes and challenges.

A robust corporate governance system makes companies more resilient to difficulties inherent in a VUCA world. A board that understands its purpose will institute a practical governance framework by setting a business strategy that considers potential risks. In addition, the board will ensure that they establish appropriate risk management and oversight systems and institutionalize decision-making processes.

When a crisis occurs (or is occurring), good corporate governance provides the impetus for an effective rebound.

Board Oversight in a VUCA World

The board and executives must first recognize that the company is facing a crisis. This first step is difficult, especially during the onset of problems that do not arrive suddenly but grow out of familiar circumstances that mask their nature.[90] Identifying a slow-developing crisis for what it might become requires boards and executives to overcome the *normalcy bias*, which can cause them to underestimate the possibility of a full-blown crisis and the impact that it could potentially have.[91]

The board should provide the CEO and executive team with guidance, support, and advice on reacting to and managing the situation during a crisis. While a crisis may necessitate an increased involvement of the board, it does not justify micromanaging. There are a few VUCA response actions that can enhance the transition from fragility to agility during a crisis:

1. *V - Visualize the desired future and work toward it.* When in a crisis, it is essential to maintain a proper perspective of the corporate goals, as it provides a good sense of direction. Taking into cognizance the ensuing crisis, what should the company's focus be for the not-too-distant future? Reframe the situation and positively anticipate the change that is evolving. Envisioning will guide board (re)composition, employee selection, retraining of employees as effort may be on new skills (such as problem-solving, critical thinking, technology, risk analysis, etc.) Visualization is reminiscent of the forward-looking dimension of the Five-Way Directional Model©.

   The board will be better positioned to provide necessary guidance and support to the CEO and the executives if it has articulated the desired direction of the business. The directors' experience and expertise allow them to bring a different perspective to the immediacy and importance of handling a crisis appropriately. Board members should be available to give guidance at any time and to communicate regularly with the executives. External advisers, such as external legal counsel or other specialists, should be retained to advise on dealing with specific challenges whenever necessary.

2. *U - Understand the dynamics.* A natural response to uncertainty is to seek and gather information. Gathering information should be aimed at providing a better understanding of the market, customers, and competition. Availability of information is critical to reducing uncertainty, but boards and executives should move beyond existing information sources to gather new data and consider it from new perspectives.[92]

   The board must understand the dynamics and require more frequent and current information on critical risk and performance indicators to protect the interests of shareholders and stakeholders during a crisis. This may include a stronger focus on liquidity, cash management, risks, and stress testing. Boards and executives need to begin with factors that are assured, aggregate these factors and plan with them. Boards must leverage the known without agonizing over the unknown. Understanding the dynamics at play promotes better decision-making. Some understanding will come through a series of trial and error (some of which may be expensive).

To ensure that directors have the most relevant information, executives must know the needed information and at what intervals. Directors, in turn, should define the required board information architecture, letting the executives know what they want to receive. The board should also be prepared to meet more often. Meetings do not have to take place in person but could and should also take the form of a video or telephone conference. Regardless of the format, directors must continue to ask pertinent questions to enrich their own understanding. And to challenge and support management in formulating strategic responses to safeguard the company's health.

3. *C - Communicate and collaborate.* Communication in a crisis is one of the most challenging tasks yet of the utmost importance in avoiding any appearance of duplicity (which kills credibility) and potential lawsuits (which can affect the license to operate or hefty fines). Therefore, a clear line of communication should be established between the company and the public.[93]

   In 2018, the two top executives, CEO Mark Zuckerberg and Chief Operating Officer Sheryl Sandberg went radio silent after the news broke during Facebook's data saga. From a governance point of view, it is important not to stay silent. The board must communicate and should do so quickly but also knowledgeably. During a crisis, everything means something, especially silence.

Deciding to keep quiet is probably the worst possible choice. Crisis experts said that Facebook's board mishandled the data scandal by not communicating relevant information within appropriate timelines.

Sadly, crisis communications from boards and executives often hit the wrong notes because of timing, context, and content. The board must ensure that there is always a consistent message and frequent updates.[94] Board communication should be transparent and form part of the broader corporate communications framework consistent with the situation. As Amy Edmondson wrote, "Transparency is the number one job for boards and executives in a crisis. Be clear what you know, what you don't know, and what you are doing to learn more about."[95] Such a period provides an opportunity to craft and communicate corporate perspectives to the various stakeholders regularly.

As a rule of thumb, during a crisis, it is better to over-communicate than under-communicate. Communication offers strategic direction for employees and keeps shareholders abreast of developments too. Communication enhances connections and relationships, even with suppliers and customers. Boards and executives must strive to cut through the noise and connect with stakeholders.

Furthermore, making communication a conversation gives room for people to explore strategies for collaboration. Effective and efficient collaboration ensures that there is an alignment between internal company operations and external happenings. In doing this, the external stakeholders are actively engaged, enabling a win-win position. In summary, communication must be clear, concise, complete, continuous, consistent, and from a credible source, the board.

4. *A - Adapt and be agile.* C. K. Prahalad, professor of corporate strategy, proposed that in a volatile world, companies should aim to become "Velcro organizations," which means that people and capacity can be rearranged and recombined creatively and quickly without a significant structural change. This is the factor that ensures that a company is enabled to pivot during a crisis. Effective boards and executives will simultaneously focus on quality, cost, and efficiency through experimentation to reduce ambiguity.

Only through intelligent experimentation can leaders determine what strategies are and are not beneficial in situations where former business rules no longer apply.[96] This is a good summation of adaptability. Boards and executives need to answer the questions, "What is our adaptability quotient (AQ)?" "What is the AQ of our employees?" "What is the AQ of our company?" The more adaptable these are, the easier it will be to rebound.

During a crisis and as executives struggle to adapt, the board is responsible for supervising the executive team's response to the crisis. Given that the board is usually more removed from the immediate crisis management, it can provide practical observation and alternative viewpoints on the actions taken by the executives. The board can also give feedback on proposed actions before their implementation. Adaptability also extends to the increased need for directors' involvement; in most cases, the number of board meetings increases significantly. A CEO said,

"In the last year, we doubled the number of board meetings, and I met weekly with the chairman and his deputy. I would not like to go through a crisis without such feedback and assurance. But I don't want to maintain this either once business is back to normal."[97]

Effective boards and executives who want their companies to survive and thrive will apply these VUCA actions (visualize, understand, communicate and collaborate, and adapt) in an intentional manner. A statement that buttresses the points above is this:

"I guess one of the reasons that my company managed the crisis relatively better than others is because we had a great leadership team and board, who listened to one another and were able to communicate throughout the organization. There were just no bad surprises due to a high level of transparency and openness." —Board director, Egypt[98]

Five Ways a Board Chair Can CHAIR in a Crisis

In the heat of the COVID-19 pandemic, I was honored to speak (virtually) at the 7th Annual Conference of the Women on Boards Network Kenya on *key areas of focus for boards in a VUCA environment.* During the Q&A session, I was asked what advice I would give to a board chair on navigating a crisis if they have never been exposed to a crisis as a board chairperson. In response to the question, I came up with these five things that a board chair can do to CHAIR the board during a crisis.

The role of the chairperson is critical to good corporate governance and the board's effective performance. The chairperson's primary function is to provide overall leadership to the board, ensuring that the board effectively sets and oversees the company's direction and crisis management strategy. The chairperson links the board and CEO/executives and should work collaboratively with the CEO.

During a crisis, the board chairperson needs to ensure that the board supports the CEO in managing crises and keeping the company afloat. It is also essential that directors give management sufficient space to take the actions required and embed the results without unnecessary intervention or an attempt to micromanage them inadvertently.

To make my recommendations memorable, I used the acronym CHAIR to describe how a board chairperson could act during a crisis to remain effective and fulfill the responsibilities.

1) **C** – Carry others along. A crisis is a confusing time, so it is crucial to gain buy-in for initiatives that should be embarked upon to respond to the situation. Getting the views and perspectives of other directors makes decisions more robust. There should be constant two-way communication between the CEO and the chairperson. There should also be constant two-way communication between the chairperson and the other board members. Effective communication ensures that all directors are informed and carried along as the situation develops.

The chairperson needs to be mindful that there could be board members with experience relevant and valuable to the CEO and executives. This consciousness may lead to assigning specific tasks to board members according to their expertise.

An African adage goes thus, "If you want to go fast, go alone; if you want to go far, go together." It may be tempting to take unilateral decisions, but involving other directors and leveraging their perspectives adds value and reduces the burden. The chairperson must create an atmosphere (even before a crisis) of "we are in this together, and if we do not hang together, we will hang separately to our detriment." As the standard-bearer for structures, processes, and behaviors, the chairperson can do a lot to reinforce more constructive, collaborative, and value-creating board work.

2) **H** – Help the board navigate the crisis. The chairperson needs to step up the direction of board work during crises. During these difficult times, the chairperson becomes a helper in multiple dimensions. He/she must

... Help the executives or fully take responsibility in discussions and negotiations with key stakeholders;

... Help the company regain its credibility by making the right decisions and taking appropriate actions;

... Help directors stay on track, taking responsibility for the board's shortcomings and adapting structures/processes accordingly;

... Help directors overcome biases and paralysis in reaction to the crisis; and

... Help the board admit failure, lenience, and sloppiness if appropriate to learn for the future.

The chairperson must also proactively seek and accept help. It is vital to have a support network. In moments of crisis and profound disruption, the top is very lonely, and a sense of isolation can quickly seem overwhelming even to the most resilient leader.

A chairperson who wants to remain effective should have a reliable support network, especially in a crisis, possibly including a coach. During times of crisis, the chairperson should also reach out to/take advantage of experts' (e.g., legal, financial, sector advisers) opinions on critical things. Leveraging experts is essential as they provide helpful input to critical strategic decisions.

3) **A** – Align every activity or initiative with the company's strategic objectives and the source of the crisis. A vital part of the chairperson's job is (re)focusing the board and executives on the big picture, reiterating the importance of the mission clearly

and consistently during a crisis, and assisting others, particularly the CEO, to be well aligned. Alignment allows for synchronized actions; directors and executives can work together, leveraging everyone's unique skills, to move efficiently toward the common goal.

Most boards decide to form a special committee during a crisis, a task force that usually includes external experts, as a crisis-response team. The chairperson should have ownership of such a formation. This is especially necessary when executives must concentrate on the continuation of normal operations.

Whatever the case may be, the chairperson must ensure that there is sufficient alignment to avoid derailing the team. The composition of a crisis-response team depends on the type of crisis, the capabilities of executives, and the corporate governance system.

4) **I** – Integrate alliances. There are several situations in which board members do not come to a board as independent entities but rather as representatives of specific stakeholder (interest) groups, creating subgroups or blocs. During a crisis, it is not uncommon that subgroup activities are more pronounced, affecting board functioning. Therefore, the chairperson must find common ground to promote integration or identify individuals who can act as bridges rather than barriers. This will prevent a rift during a crisis that could affect the board's functioning and negatively impact the company.

Apart from integrating internal alliances, efforts should be made to integrate external alliances (stakeholder groups). Having good relations and a communication pattern between the board and the company's stakeholders before a crisis is always an advantage. The problem with poor stakeholder relations during a crisis is that there are limited foundations on which the board can garner support for its actions, and making new friends in a crisis can be difficult. Hopefully, therefore, the chairperson was astute at managing these alliances in good times.

Regarding ED vs. NED faction, the vital question is whether the board has dominated management or vice versa in time past. Such power relationships do not necessarily change in a crisis but instead can be intensified. Regardless of the state of relationships, though, it makes sense to draw a quick "map" to understand the complexity of interrelations and interdependencies between these factions, be they internal or external stakeholders and among the different stakeholders themselves. A dominant executive team might even completely ignore the board in a crisis, or an overbearing board might tend to micromanage even more. Therefore, the role of the chairperson in integrating divergent interests is critical.

5) **R** – Relax. Remain calm and stay focused. Take a deep breath and exhale. Studies show that it is common for boards and executives to react poorly in a crisis. An interesting piece of board and leadership research revealed that 53 percent of boards and executives become more closed-minded and controlling during a crisis instead of open and curious; 43 percent become angrier and more irritable.

A chairperson cannot control anything if he/she does not first exercise self-control. Staying calm allows one to think creatively and correctly. Remain calm. I like the quote: "Staying cool, calm, and collected during times of stress is a must. Figuring out how to do it is a continual challenge." This is the challenge that the chair must overcome.

The Role of Independent Directors in a Crisis

The strength of a board is tested when the board faces a crisis. During times of crisis, the stakes are higher, and scrutiny is more intense, the board must strengthen their governance functions, and relationship with executives in fighting for survival and ensuring that the company emerges from the crisis more robust and resilient

During crises, regulators often look to the independent director to provide objective information. The point about the independent directors is that they are drawn from a pool of professionals who have had broad industry experience and are qualified to sit on the boards of the companies. This concept appeals to the regulators because independent directors can bring objective and balanced perspectives since they are not connected to the company nor its management and hence do not (or should not) have hidden agendas.

Typically, independent directors bring fresh perspectives and check the runaway business behavior dictated by profits and personal benefit. The independent directors are the ones who often prevent the executives from making decisions that are based on personal benefits as opposed to the interests of the company. Further, independent directors are tasked with investigating cases of corporate malfeasance and unethical behavior because of their supposed objectivity and neutrality.

However, there have been instances where the independent directors themselves acquiesced in the companies' wrongdoings and their boards. The solution to this has been the initiative to make the independent directors responsible for the board's actions so that they have a stake in ensuring that the board does not tread on the wrong side, particularly during a crisis.

In November 2018[99], The New York Times ran a front-page story describing how Facebook covered up knowledge and disclosure of Russian-linked activity and exploitation, resulting in Kremlin-led disruption of the 2016 and 2018 U.S. elections, using global hate campaigns and propaganda warfare. This crisis progressed quickly; the backlash from political leaders and the media posed a severe governance challenge as it kept the spotlight on the board and executives, particularly the CEO. The shareholders and the board had to figure out what to do.

The board was urged to tighten oversight by creating a privacy committee composed of independent directors in the final analysis. The bottom line for independent directors is that their responsibilities and obligations are so vital that they cannot serve on a board and expect to preside while fulfilling the minimum requirements. Instead, they need to be fully engaged, learn the business, and stay connected between meetings. Otherwise, they will not be prepared to lead when a crisis hits, which is inevitable.

Globally, regulators have moved in many countries to ensure that independent directors do not have conflicts of interest. These have been codified into rules governing how many companies they can associate themselves with and the sectors and industries they represent. Independent directors have a critical role in maintaining board discipline, being objective, and exercising good judgment under the chairperson's guidance and leadership.

Quick Check: Questions for Boards and Executives

These questions were drawn mainly from the tip sheet for company leadership on crisis response developed by the International Finance Corporation (IFC).[100] The questions should be asked during a crisis or if the board wants to confirm that the company is prepared for a crisis (a risk management function).

- Is the board demonstrating leadership during the crisis, communicating clearly and on time to employees and key stakeholders?

- Has the board checked/reviewed the business continuity plan (BCP) to determine if it contemplates the current scenario? If not, consider immediately updating BCP.
- Does the board monitor compliance with BCP policies and procedures, ensuring that the compliance team knows how to escalate issues in real-time with direct access to the board?
- Is the board able to hold emergency or ad hoc board meetings in the event of a crisis?
- Is the board risk management committee appropriately composed to oversee the impacts and management of crisis?
- Is there an open discussion on whether the board has the capacity and skills to oversee the BCP and lead the company through the crisis?
- Does the company have a succession plan, and is it ready to be activated?
- Is there a comprehensive plan to address crisis impacts under different potential scenarios? The plan should be relative to the intensity and duration of the crisis and its possible effects on liquidity, funding, key business lines, and supply chains.
- How are impacts of a crisis on the workforce reported to the board?
- Are the critical control functions functioning well? Consider:
- Internal Controls: adequacy of BCP policies and procedures, IT controls related to telecommuting, workplace safety, food safety, etc. Don't overlook Cyber/IT issues. In times of crisis, these vulnerabilities may be worsened.
- Compliance: adequacy of compliance with relevant controls, including but not limited to BCP, IT, safety, etc.
- Internal Audit: capacity for alternative procedures for continuing the audit work plan and reporting, assessing the adequacy of BCP, advising on deficiencies of related controls, and corrective action.
- Risk Management: risk assessments and mitigants for related immediate risks as well as long-term implications.

CHAPTER 8

THE BOARD AND DIGITALIZATION

How boards of directors deal with the impact of digitalization may determine whether or not their companies will be competitive in the future. The board plays a vital role for the company to adapt to the changing strategic context [101]. Digital transformation is a pressing concern for executives and boards in every industry, yet one in which respondents in a 2020 Heidrick & Struggles survey on the board of the future do not see boards taking a leading role[102]. This begs the question, "Are todays' boards adequately equipped to create value for companies in the future?"

Although the increased pace of digitization is cited as the most significant challenge facing traditional companies, very few see boards taking a leading role in digital transformation in the short to medium term.

At the fourteenth EIASM workshop on corporate governance in Brussels, Belgium (mentioned in the introduction), a couple of researchers (Hugh Grove, Laura Georg, and Mac Clouse) also presented a paper titled "Digitalization Impacts on Corporate Governance."[103] I found the paper presented very insightful. After the presentation, I spent time poring over the data provided. Digitalization is a significant influencer of business success.

Digitalization is no longer just a buzzword. It enables companies to compete more effectively in the ever-changing digital economy, yet it instills fear and apprehension in many directors.[104] Directors need to understand how digital transformation can enable success and their role in its implementation. Interestingly, digitalization is another area where boards must adopt the entire Five-Way Directional Model©. Boards should look -

1. Forward, strategically, and envision future digital goals for business advancement.
2. Backward, retrospectively, contemplating experiences with old methods and models. It is essential to consider the lessons learned from past digitalization initiatives and establish the best way forward.
3. Inward, reflectively, assessing the digital skills on the board and how to enhance the board's digital capacity.
4. Outward and establish how the needs of stakeholders can be better served, and seeking opportunities to collaborate effectively on digital initiatives; and
5. Upward, soberly, and ethically, becoming a good corporate citizen and ensuring that technological innovations are ethically adopted and implemented.

#Digitalization - the New Normal

If a board is not bothered about digital,
I will sell my shares in that company!
—Brian McBride, Chairman, Asos[105]

To understand how digitalization impacts the role and functioning of boards, it is necessary first to define and know how it can enable new business models. According to Gartner[106], digitalization is the use of digital technologies to change a business model and provide new revenue and value-producing opportunities; it is the process of moving to a digital business that transforms a business's operating model.

In chapter 7, I mentioned the opportunity to speak at the Women on Boards Network's virtual conference on *key areas of focus for boards in a VUCA environment*. One of the key areas of focus for boards is *Digital Disruption*. Boards are responsible for ensuring that digitalization can unlock productivity gains and significant competitive advantage while delivering strong business results.

At the 2016 World Economic Forum meeting in Davos, Switzerland, some influential leaders advocated developing a digital mindset that understands the potential, the disruptive nature, and the risks associated with digitalization. They stressed that a company's ability to harness the benefits of digitalization could drive profitability, offer critical insights, and open new business opportunities.

Developing a digital mindset meant that boards should embrace and support management to provide new revenue and value-producing opportunities. It is only a matter of time before digital technology becomes like electricity, as a seamless part of our daily lives and the operations of every business. Therefore, boards of the future must understand and embrace digitalization to enhance value for the companies they lead.

The world has experienced unprecedented technological advancements in the past eighteen months, fueled by COVID-19 and the lockdown. The way people shop, bank, relate, work and live has changed due to the pandemic. Technology plays an essential role in *the new normal,* ensuring that business activities are contactless and can continue safely. These safety measures include using QR codes in restaurants and hotels to order food, capacity control through the digitization of physical spaces, virtual meetings and conferences, remote temperature sensors, and leveraging Big Data and Artificial Intelligence in decision making. Digital transformation is changing how businesses operate in many ways, including how board members engage with each other and executives.

Digitalization is a central issue, as shown by the KPMG report[107] "CEO Outlook 2020: COVID-19." Eighty percent of the CEOs of the world's largest organizations say the pandemic has accelerated digital transformation, with the most significant advance in digital operations. Thirty percent say that this progress has put them years ahead of where they expected to be right now. In another study of 2,549 corporate decision-makers in June 2020 conducted by Twillo[108], 96 percent of leaders believe the pandemic sped up their digital transformation by an average of 5.3 years.

"The post-COVID-19 era will bring forward a new normal – one that will accelerate digital transformation in many areas," said Liu Zhenmin, UN Under-Secretary-General and Head of United Nations Department of Economic and Social Affairs (UN DESA). "These include digital economy, digital finance, digital government, digital health, and digital education." These statements were made at the 2020 Annual Meeting of the Internet Governance Forum of UN DESA and buttress a global perspective.

Digitalization is not just about technology innovations and how they disrupt the business. It is also about how directors and executives adopt and use these technological innovations to add value to the company.

Governance of the Fourth Industrial Revolution (4IR),

There is a wave of innovations in today's fast-changing business environment, and many customer behaviors, habits, and expectations have shifted. Undoubtedly digitalization will play a huge role in the future of business. But how can boards and executives tap into these technologies for strategic advantage? To gain strategic perspective, nearly a dozen CEOs came together to discuss the Fourth Industrial Revolution (4IR) in an event hosted by the Global Lighthouse Network, a World Economic Forum (WEF) initiative in collaboration with McKinsey & Company. They provided insight on what it will take to build workforce capabilities and ignite a broader digital transformation.

These emerging technologies of 4IR, such as artificial intelligence (AI), mobility (including autonomous vehicles), blockchain, drones, and the Internet of Things (IoT), have been at the center of the innovations[109].

Some examples of the digital disruptions McKinsey once warned about are described below:

- *Disruptive applications:* Amazon is reinventing the grocery-store business model. In Seattle, it tested a grocery-store model that works without checkout lines. Shoppers can scan a new app called Amazon Go when they enter the store, and sensors register items chosen by shoppers and automatically charge them to the Amazon app.
- *Artificial intelligence (AI):* Digitalization with AI is poised to reinvent computing itself. In November 2016, Google Translate, the company's machine-translation app, significantly improved after being converted to an AI-based system.[110] When AI is

thoughtfully applied, it can enable a massive leap over standard approaches in terms of delivery speeds, costs, and quality, often by a factor of 10. This allows companies to test new markets, products, and business models at much greater speeds and lower costs.

- *Distributed ledger technology, the blockchain:* A technology expert commented, "In Distributed Ledger Technology (DLT), we may be witnessing one of those potential explosions of creative potential that catalyze exceptional levels of innovation."[111] DLT first showed its disruptive nature in developing blockchain technology in the financial sector, competing with national-governed currencies worldwide.

- *Three-dimensional printing:* In the 1980s, 3D printing, also called additive manufacturing (AM), was created as a faster and more cost-effective method for creating product prototypes. Recent technology improvements have expanded the type of printable materials to include plastics, metal, nylon, plaster, ceramics, food, and even human tissue cells.[112]

- *The Internet of things:* The Internet of things (IoT) comprises billions of everyday wireless devices that communicate with each other over the Internet and send helpful information to businesses and consumers, i.e., digitizing the physical world. For example, radio-frequency identification tags will replace the need for physical inventory counts, and automated systems can detect, predict, and prevent potential errors.[113]

- *Financial accounting:* In their book, *The End of Accounting*, Baruch Lev and Feng Gu argued that archaic accounting methods poorly serve investors and that new ways to measure companies' performance are needed. One unique way is a digital dashboard for company executives and boards. The authors stated that traditionally reported earnings and financial statements no longer reflect the realities of businesses and that new metrics are needed for "new economy" companies, such as technology, software, biotech, and Internet operators.[114]

- *Digital dashboards:* As advocated by McKinsey and Lev/ Gu, a recommended solution is the systematic disclosure of information that focuses upon the fundamentals of the business in this age of digitalization. Instead of the backward-oriented financial accounting statements, there are many forward-looking indicators of performance and growth that emphasize a business's strategy and execution success, as well as its risks.[115]

All these digital disruptions translate into a suite of technologies and capabilities poised to slip through gaps in governance. So, what are boards and executives doing about these emerging digital advances and applications? Are they seizing opportunities to create competitive advantages? Are they adapting their business models and strategies? How are today's boards ensuring that executives create competitive advantages with these opportunities while also dealing with the related risks?

At the board level, decisions must be made regarding processes, organizational measures, and technologies required in compliance with external and internal regulations.[116] As described earlier, the board plays a critical role in guaranteeing the successful transformation of the enterprise in the digital world.[117] This role calls for increased awareness and dedicated board attention and competency around technology. This is a precarious era for directors because policymakers do not have a coherent theory of the phenomenon, and there are no well-articulated set of regulatory guidelines.[118]

Digital transformation will continue to affect organizations in many ways, and its full impact, especially on boards, is not yet known. As one director mentioned, some boards have not yet broached this subject of digitalization as it relates to how the board itself operates. The onus is on boards and management to be proactive in understanding how digitalization can affect their responsibilities in scope and execution. Before future digital solutions are adopted or implemented, what should boards do better to understand the impacts of digital transformation on the governance processes?

- Gain more knowledge about the current technologies in place and new technologies on the horizon.
- Task appropriate board committees with identifying the risks and the rewards of applying these new technologies to board operations.
- Be clear on what problems you are trying to solve. Avoid the temptation to implement shiny new object technologies that may not be most effective for the issue at hand.
- Work with management to define the boundary between oversight and decision-making in the implementation of new technologies.
- When the appropriate technology tools are identified for implementation, set up proper training mechanisms to get board members up to speed.
- Develop guidelines that will help management identify the most pertinent pieces of information to share with the board, allowing board members to make the best use of their time.
- Engage in dialogue with industry associations about digitizing board processes.

Building the Board's Digital Competency

As described above, the rapid evolution of the Fourth Industrial Revolution (4IR) has enormous implications for both boards and executives as their duties in overseeing and managing their companies have become significantly more challenging. Successful digitalization in any company cannot occur without strong digital competency. Therefore, it is no surprise that a lack of digital-savvy and training around the impact of emerging digital tools, technologies, and business models is a challenge for boards.

According to Dr Jidenma, who wrote the foreword to this book "digital transformation has to do with a whole range of change management processes that includes intersection and integration of the various aspects digitalization." Arguably, the executive team is expected to take ownership of digital transformation while the board guides and offers expertise where appropriate. However, there is an overall perspective that the board lacks the necessary capabilities and experience to provide oversight of digital transformation initiatives. Today, more than ever, companies need directors who are digitally competent and understand the new technologies that are impacting business decisions.

Digitalization can change business models by removing costs and wastes and accelerating a company's pace of operations. According to a McKinsey report,[119] many boards do not fully understand that digitalization poses enormous pressures and challenges to their existing business models. Ideally, boards should do the following,

- Encourage executives to explore and expand the company's digital assets.
- Question how executives leverage these digital assets to enhance corporate performance.
- Help executives manage the tension between "making the numbers" each quarter and long-term digital investments for strategic purposes.
- Challenge executives concerning the company's traditional high costs and low flexibility, which places them at a disadvantage with digital competitors who can easily set up online marketplaces and sell directly to customers.

To be able to support executives and ask pertinent questions, the board must be digitally competent. A 2021 *Harvard Business Review* article, *"5 Questions Boards Should Be Asking about Digital Transformation,"* presents the case of the CEO of a large retail company who brought a $500 million digital transformation investment plan to his board. The board reviewed the proposal, but after asking a few questions, they could not evaluate it. Was it too costly? Was it aiming too low? Was it focused on the right priorities? One board member admitted he just didn't know.[120] This story is not new or strange, as similar scenes have played out in boardrooms worldwide for years.

Here are ways to help boards build their digital competency.

1. Recruiting the right directors with appropriate digital skills
2. Investing in continuous education for existing directors to close the knowledge gaps
3. Appoint digitalization experts and board advisors

1. *Recruiting the right directors with appropriate digital skills*

In a Harvard Business Review, the authors quoted Caroline Raggett, Managing Director for a Hong Kong-based leadership advisory, who commented that "The super-fast evolution of technology drives exponential complexity in understanding and dealing with this topic as a board. As a result, we have seen demand for digital or technology-oriented board directors more than double in the last five years[121]." According to Heidrick & Struggles' Board Monitor Europe 2019, there has been a significant rise of digital and cybersecurity skills in new director appointments to European boards[122].

It is important to appreciate that many digital directors are younger, maybe even "geeks," who have no other board experience. Thus, board searches must go beyond background and skills to include candidates' temperament and ability to commit time, especially with better board members now devoting two or three days a month of work plus extra hours for conference calls and other tasks.

Induction and onboarding processes need to bridge the digital-traditional gap or possibly create an advisory role for digital experts. Also, existing board members need to increase their digital skills to help company executives think about, cope with, and adapt to these digitalization challenges. Such digital skills can be learned by board members, who are experienced, competent people.

In a particular case, a retailer looking to speed up its digital enablement brought an executive onto the board who had recently done exactly that for another retailer, upturning an industry in the process. Another retailer looking to integrate better the digital logistics of its e-commerce and brick-and-mortar operations targeted someone with precisely that top-management experience and expertise.

2. *Investing in continuous education for existing directors to close the knowledge gaps*

Since digitalization significantly impacts a company's business model, value chain, and competitive environment, more knowledge and experience are needed than just one or two digital directors.

Michael Gourlay, board director and Chairman of the Asia division of insurance giant QBE, commented that "As organizations look to rebound in a profoundly shifting business environment, there is no turnkey solution or off-the-shelf playbook for how boards should uphold strong corporate governance, assert successful oversight, and fulfill their fiduciary duties." He further indicated that "Continuous board training is essential to equip our directors with new skills and up-to-date expertise in key areas such as stakeholder engagement, compliance, audits, diversity, sustainability, cybersecurity, and risk management." Thomas Freidman said that lifelong jobs require lifelong learning. Indeed, in the spirit of lifelong learning, directors need to develop digital skills without becoming, or just relying upon, digitalization experts.

Some interesting facts emerged from a study of almost 800 global board directors conducted by the professional services firm Tricor Group and the Financial Times Board Director Programme. One of these facts is that "while 94 percent of surveyed directors said they felt they needed more training on new technology and governance best practices, just 58 percent reported receiving that training."

3. *Appoint digitalization experts and board advisors*

Another way to build the board's digital competency is to leverage the expertise of external advisors or consultants. The Tricor Group study mentioned above indicated that "just 48 percent of global directors said they would consider employing independent, third-party expertise from corporate governance advisors, consultants, and cybersecurity experts to develop those critical digital governance competencies."

Interestingly, the research found that directors in countries where confidence levels were the highest (Japan, China, and Singapore) were more interested in engaging external expertise and advisors, suggesting a correlation between investment in training programs (and seeking expert advisors) and more confident crisis response."

Arguably, these efforts have a price tag, which could be hefty. It can be challenging to dedicate the necessary time and budget when the company faces many other challenges. But now more than ever, boards cannot afford not to build these critical digital competencies — either through informal briefings, workshops, or formal advisory services.

The widespread adoption of new digital solutions over the last few years has accelerated the need for boards to think differently about digitalization. It would be "up to the board to make sure that an organization is fulfilling its mission and making a meaningful, lasting impact on the customers and communities it serves. That means investing in digital tools, following cybersecurity best practices, and developing the skills required to support a company in today's digital-first world[123]."

Digital Board Governance Infrastructure

Before the COVID-19 pandemic, only about 5 percent of board meetings were conducted online/virtually. In the heat of the pandemic, between 2020 and mid-2021, the number of online/virtual board meetings increased to 95 percent. Research indicates that even post-COVID-19, more than 50 percent of boards will pursue a hybrid (simultaneously physical and virtual) meeting model.

As described in chapter 1 (Where Do and When Should Boards Meet?), physical/in-person board meetings have advantages. However, data from Tricor Group suggests that finding the right balance between online/virtually and physical/in-person board meetings (i.e., hybrid) can significantly increase the efficiency of board meetings. Hybrid board meetings tend to result in almost 30 percent shorter meetings with 20 percent higher attendance[124]. Therefore, the hybrid model for board meetings is a viable option for boards of the future. A hybrid meeting model creates the need to leverage digital tools for board operations.

I once partnered with Ralph Hohls, the head of OnBoard Africa, to run a webinar on the opportunity for boards to hold strategic and super-efficient board meetings with real-time collaboration. The Onboard board management technology platform helps boards to accomplish more inside and outside of the boardroom. According to Ralph Hohls, OnBoard is a virtual board management solution that securely connects companies and their directors to meeting materials, agendas, minutes, approvals, eSignatures, calendars, policies, and procedures. He tells me that OnBoard is trusted by more than 12,000 boards of directors and committees worldwide, including public companies, private organizations, non-profit organizations, and government bodies. There are several other platforms with similar offerings. It would appear as if new ones emerge each day.

Despite the necessity of digital board governance tools in an increasingly hybrid world and the plethora of digital board governance tools available, many boards are still using general tools such as Google Meet, Zoom, or WeChat for virtual meetings rather than systems specifically designed for digital board governance.

A typical digital board governance infrastructure supports vital board-specific processes such as sharing secure governance documents, voting or communicating confidential information. Ralph Hohls indicates that there is a strong interest in leveraging digital tools to support board operations.

A Harvard Business Review article by Diana Wu David and Sunshine Farzan (Boards Are Undergoing Their Own Digital Transformation) describes the COVID-19-enabled transition to virtual board meetings. "During the pandemic, we had board members stuck overseas in Singapore and the United Kingdom, and even before Covid-19, getting signatures for things like board resolutions was always a pain," explained Jo Hayes, CEO of Habitat for Humanity Hong Kong. "Switching to digital was an absolute game-changer. It reduced all the administrative costs associated with board meetings and tasks related to circulating board papers."

Boards of the future will do well to adopt and adequately implement appropriate digital board governance infrastructure to boost the efficiency of board operations.

Emerging Risk Management Challenges

Cybersecurity risks change with every new digital invention introduced, adding potential threats. Cybersecurity risks are usually specific to a company's business model and values. The proof of any board's successful digital transformation is the board's ability to address emerging cybersecurity risks. Boards that invest in operational tools without adequately addressing the increased cybersecurity threats that come with those tools expose themselves and their companies to significant risk. While cybersecurity has long been on many boards' radars, the combination of widespread distributed work and increasingly sophisticated attackers in the past year has expanded both opportunities for attacks and the impact of these attacks on business activities.

Exposure to cybersecurity threats and vulnerability must be regularly reassessed and organized in meaningful categories, such as security risks compromising the business processes, client-facing activities, or support functions. Typically, these areas should be separated into logical IT-architectural domains to help boards understand the business impact of IT-security risks.[125]

Another emerging risk for hacks and data breaches is related to the Internet of things (IoT). A study by Hewlett Packard found that 70 percent of the most commonly used IoT devices contain vulnerabilities. A global study by Ernst & Young found that 56 percent of corporate executives said that it is unlikely that their organizations would detect a sophisticated attack.[126] For example, hackers attacked the IoT in 2016. One day in March, $81 million of Bangladesh's money disappeared from its account at the Federal Reserve Bank of New York. The hackers accessed the SWIFT international bank messaging system, "billed as a super-secure system that banks use to authorize payments." In contrast, it took the famous U.S. bank robber Willie Sutton forty years to steal $2 million.[127]

Digital transformation depends on networks that are often shared and do not follow typical geographical or industrial silos, such as Industry 4.0 technology for a value or supply chain. Networks can be shared around the world and cover all types of clients. At the same time, if these networks are infected, such infections can spread widely and affect the business of the entire network.

An infection in a cloud provider with an international customer base offering virtualization technology would affect all such customers equally. For example, an infected insurance company on the cloud could be facing an accumulation of claims that could threaten its survival and might eliminate individual customers' insurance coverage. Discovering these hidden interrelationships between companies generates a new form of assessment, including further questions covering such interconnectivity risks.[128]

For improved corporate governance in this age of digitalization, the board needs to investigate critical operating performance indicators or KPIs for competitive advantage. While the awareness on boards regarding risks originating from disruptive innovation, cyber threats, and privacy risks has been increasing, board members must equally be able to challenge executives and identify opportunities and threats for their companies.

Companies now face unprecedented vulnerability to cyberattacks that can threaten sensitive information and disrupt business. This shift for companies is not only about digital technology but also culture. How can people be managed when digital, virtual ways of working are increasing? What do robotics and "big data" analysis mean for managing people? As one executive put it, "Digital is what we're going to be doing for the rest of our lives." The urgency and longevity that underlie that statement make supporting a successful digital transformation a priority for boards. As the pressures and complexities of digitalization increase, boards have a pivotal role in guiding their institutions through successful long-term digital transformation.

The board's oversight on cybersecurity is more critical today than ever before. While there is no one-size-fits-all approach, boards can mitigate these growing risks and instill a culture of security throughout the organization by creating a dedicated cybersecurity committee, establishing board-level oversight on cybersecurity issues, and holding regular security briefings

Quick Check: Questions for Boards and Executives

According to the *Harvard Business Review* article[129] referred to above, asking the following questions will ensure that boards are focused on the most critical digital challenges. Some questions have also been adapted from Mckinsey's article[130] "Five Questions Boards Should Ask About IT in a Digital World." While some of these questions are more strategic and others more operational, boards and executives that can address all of them can help companies achieve the digital transformation goals essential to today's business competitive advantage.

- Is the corporate digital plan increasing the business or technology agility?
- Does the board understand the implications of digital and technology well enough to provide valuable guidance?
- Is the digital transformation fundamentally changing how the business (and sector) creates value?
- How well does technology enable the core business?
- Is your board asking the right questions about AI, blockchain, new technology, and cyber security to help ensure long-term success for the business?
- Is technology helping the company win against the competition?
- What value is the business getting from its most important digitalization projects?
- How does the board know if the digital transformation is working?
- Does the board have a sufficiently expansive view of digital talent?
- Do your board members request cybersecurity risk and planning updates from the IT department, conduct

third-party cybersecurity audits, or get involved in the company's cybersecurity threat response simulations?

- Does the board have a clear view of emerging risks and opportunities?
- How long does it take the IT organization to develop and deploy new features and functionality?
- How efficient is IT at rolling out technologies and achieving desired outcomes?
- Do you have the right technology skills to deliver the technology innovation you need for growth?
- How strong is the supply of next-generation IT talent?
- What skills do you need most on the board to meet your digital transformation plan?
- What opportunities exist to enhance board effectiveness through digital technologies?

CHAPTER 9

DYSFUNCTIONAL BOARDS

I have worked with boards of various sizes in all sectors for several years, and (sadly) most of them exhibit some degree of dysfunctionality. Sometimes the board is aware, and at other times they are completely oblivious about their state. Many of the corporate failures that have made headlines in recent years can be traced to board dysfunctionality.

Jay W. Lorsch agrees that legal and regulatory requirements bring boards together, and the board's focus is typically on financial and strategic matters. However, he opines that *"at the most basic level, they are groups of experienced part-timers from many different careers who come together to govern a company. Getting such groups to function as an effective governing body is, if nothing else, a challenge in establishing and sustaining effective human relationships, not only among board members but also between the board and its top management, especially its CEO.*[131]*"*

Dysfunctionality 101

A board is dysfunctional when it fails to perform its primary duty, which is to make appropriate decisions and provide the executives with the proper strategic guidance. A dysfunctional board causes multiple problems for the company. Not only will a dysfunctional board often fail to make decisions that are in the best interest of the company, but its dysfunctionality also has the potential to move outside the confines of the boardroom, causing negative publicity.

Board dysfunctionality is challenging to identify and understand; it can be elusive and not readily acknowledged. Such behavior is rarely overt and dramatic such as with raised voices, direct threats, personal defensiveness, or sullen silence. Instead, it plays out more subtly through furtive glances, vague innuendo, closed questioning, quiet acquiescence, intellectual gameplaying, awkward standoffs, and silent withdrawals. Unfortunately, less-observant directors will deny that anything is wrong, thereby accommodating and perpetuating the behavior. More reflective directors will know what this feels like and how it impacts their board's effectiveness.

The boardroom itself is changing, and dysfunctionality may be even harder to identify today than was the case previously. Remote board meetings have increased since the pandemic. Directors may no longer see or sense their colleague's reluctance to contribute or a peer's controlling nature or other forms of emotional tensions experienced in face-to-face interactions, but they still operate behind the scenes. In dysfunctional board meetings, the smooth civility on the surface often belies the ongoing turbulence beneath.

I have found that when a board becomes dysfunctional, the problem is often with the board's composition. People are appointed directors because of their expertise, experience, reputations, networks, and strong personalities. This mix can create its own challenges. Issues can also arise when people are not remunerated appropriately or are there on a volunteer basis, so it becomes a lower priority for them.

Knowing the signs of a dysfunctional board of directors can be beneficial and prevent the catastrophe that can evolve.

Tensions in the Boardroom

As directors work together and evolve into a functional group, there are sometimes unavoidable tensions. Directors and executives must contend with and manage these tensions to improve working relationships or degenerate into dysfunctionality. Depending on the situation, managing tensions is an art that directors need to master over time. In an article, Katharina Pick and Kenneth Merchant identified some tensions inherent in the functioning of most boards.

Social-Cohesion Tension

Social cohesion is defined as the willingness of members of a group to cooperate with one another to survive and prosper. Willingness to cooperate means they freely choose to form partnerships and have a reasonable chance of realizing their individual and collective goals.[132] In the boardroom, there is usually a tension between creating social cohesion and avoiding it.

Strong social cohesion allows the board to function smoothly and keeps the directors motivated. However, social cohesion can also heighten pressures of conformity on directors (peer pressure). An overly cohesive and chummy board is described as "the old boys' club." The more socially cohesive the board is, the greater the pressure for directors to conform to the majority's point of view. Conformity can prevent divergent views and opinions from emerging, leading to groupthink.

If the board does not manage this tension between being cohesive and avoiding it, the fallout is likely either destructive conflict or groupthink. In the book Digitizing Boardroom, Pearl Zhu wrote, "Group thinking" or lack of courage to ask the tough and strategic questions is the chief weakness of Boards today.[133]"

Dissension Tension

The noun "dissension" is typically used for situations where people cannot agree or get along.[134]

Another tension is the degree to which dissent should exist or even be encouraged in board discussions. On the one hand, disagreement or simply expressing an alternative viewpoint is critical to avoiding conformity. Research shows that merely considering a minority viewpoint allows a board to think more creatively and make better decisions.

However, too much dissent can create conflict, undermine the group's cohesion, and stall meetings, leading to infighting and chaos. This manifests in a lack of respect, trust, and openness, with an antagonistic atmosphere. A board that is constantly disagreeing cannot deliver on its responsibilities effectively and efficiently.

Psychological-Safety Tension

Psychological safety is about creating a safe place for risk-taking, sharing unpopular ideas, and admitting errors, which invites curiosity and learning.[135] When the board chairperson creates an environment of psychological safety, members are more likely to speak up, ask questions, and admit mistakes. These are important to other board outcomes, such as decision-making and learning. Having psychological safety counteracts conformity pressures and groupthink and can keep a board from following an unexamined habitual routine.

However, too much safety can create a tendency toward social loafing. Social loafing occurs when individuals engaged in a collective task exert less effort than they would if they were performing this task alone. Social loafing could manifest in directors showing up to meetings unprepared and instances of weak or lack of participation.

Establishing the right balance is therefore essential.

Diversity Tension

I have done a lot of work on board composition, selection, and succession and can safely say that board diversity is good for business. In academic literature, diversity is often referred to as a double-edged sword, meaning it can have positive and negative effects. In terms of positive attributes, diversity brings different perspectives to the board, ultimately leading to better decision-making. These different perspectives may refer to different world views, approaches to problem-solving, and variations in market-specific knowledge. Therefore it portends well for the business.

On the flip side, in terms of negative attributes, diversity can create communication difficulties and may lead to personality clashes. Differences in points of view may be interpreted as personal attacks or the promotion of hidden agendas, leading to reduced effort and commitment to the group. In addition, diversity may reduce trust. These negative aspects of diversity make boards less efficient.

Therefore, as good as the diversity agenda is, an overly diverse board is less likely to be highly socially cohesive or effective. This tension has to be carefully managed to forestall any form of dysfunctionality.

Strong-Leader Tension

Board leaders, either chairpersons or lead independent directors, have important roles to fill. They must be in charge and lead the board's activities. They must shape the board meeting norms and culture, set the agendas, and frame the issues appropriately. At times they must be firm and not allow, for example, time to be wasted or debate to get out of control.

Boards need strong, but not too strong, leadership. In being strong, board leaders must be careful not to alienate directors or upset the balance of power in a "board of equals." They must encourage each board member to contribute their knowledge and perspectives. And, of course, the board leaders must be careful not to exploit their power by having their opinions prevail. Although convictions can be strong, the board must govern as a collective.

When the varying tensions above are either unacknowledged or not properly managed, they degenerate into a state of dysfunctionality with symptoms as described below.

Signs of Dysfunctionality

To paraphrase Tolstoy's *Anna Karenina*, "While all happy boards are alike; each unhappy board is unhappy in its own way." There are many signs of a dysfunctional board, and it would be impossible to cover every known scenario. Sometimes board dysfunctionality may revolve around a relatively easily fixed matter, and at other times, there are much bigger issues at stake. The common reasons a board is dysfunctional include one or more of the following:

1. *Board size.* Too few or too many directors can pose problems for effective decision-making. A board with too few members may not allow the company to benefit from an appropriate mix

of skills and experience. On the other hand, a larger board is typically more challenging to manage and can make consensus-building time-consuming and difficult.

2. *Board mix.* While board size is important, board performance can be impaired when it lacks the right combination of director skills, experience, and valuable attributes. The composition should depend on the industry and the company's particular circumstances, considering the strategic direction.

3. *Poorly-structured committees.* Some boards do not have an appropriate number of board committees to help focus and provide greater scrutiny on particular issues. The number and types of committees will vary by company and industry. Failure to set up appropriate board committees and formally define their roles and responsibilities can create confusion or leave issues uncovered.

4. *Lack of confidentiality.* Much of what the board discusses should be kept within the company. Board meetings are settings where open and candid discussions should be had. Hence, confidentiality is of the utmost importance and must always be maintained. It is disheartening when details of confidential board conversations are heard in the corridors by people who do not need to know. To ensure complete discreetness, board members should sign a code of ethics and confidentiality statements upon assuming a seat on the board.

5. *Inadequate information provided.* There are cases where the board does not receive accurate, complete, reliable, relevant, and timely information. Insufficient information limits the ability of the board to make the right decisions. Often boards have not defined the information the executives should provide. Without clear directives from the board, they are at the mercy of the executives. When this happens, the board only sees what they are presented with and can easily become passive recipients of agendas created by powerful CEOs and senior executives.

6. *Conflicting focus.* Directors need to be on the same page regarding the future and strategic direction of a company and its initiatives. If directors have conflicting ideas relating to the company's strategic direction, it will be difficult for the board to make the right decisions. In addition to being on the same page, directors must also be on the same page with the executives.

7. *Preoccupation with procedures.* When a board becomes overly preoccupied with procedural matters and worries more about mundane practices than the significant issues its company faces, the board is clearly not acting in the company's best interest. There are instances where boards spend an excessive portion of the board meeting correcting the minutes of the previous meeting without any valuable additions.

8. *Unprepared directors.* Board members have a fiduciary responsibility to be prepared and to make meaningful contributions at every board meeting. In not doing so, they cannot demonstrate that they have reviewed meeting material in advance and are ready to discuss each agenda item. Most importantly, they will not be able to provide a rationale for supporting or not supporting board recommendations or actions.

9. *Lack of respect, trust, and openness.* Directors can disagree but still respect one another. When civility breaks down, infighting begins, and a board can be split into antagonistic factions. Sometimes it is a lack of respect between new and old directors; sometimes, directors experience a lack of respect from the company's CEO and vice versa. What distinguishes exemplary boards is that they are robust, effective social systems.

10. *Antagonistic atmosphere.* When directors do not get along with one another for whatever reason, it creates a hostile environment. This type of environment stifles productivity and prevents directors from sharing constructive opinions. A meeting may become a venue for personal attacks rather than focusing on business decisions or providing productive discourse. The

highest-performing companies have extremely contentious boards that regard dissent as an obligation and treat no subject as undiscussable but without personal attacks.

11. *Secret (off-the-record) meetings.* Board meetings should be scheduled for all directors to attend and share their views. Off-the-record meetings mean that small inner groups make decisions outside of the board meeting. Some directors will be left out of secret meetings, and decisions could be made without the input of crucial board members or with unethical motives. Incidentally, this is quite common and deserves a little more scrutiny. Some people believe it is a good thing and helps build consensus. To take decisions in secret meetings is a subversion of the directors' duties.

12. *Personal (hidden) agenda.* Individuals who accept a board appointment should do so to advance the company's goals. Hence, they offer their time, expertise, professional network, and unique talents solely for that purpose. A board seat should never be sought to advance one's personal, political, or business agenda. If board members continually propose moves that would benefit them personally or take a political stance, the company's image could be compromised. Personal and political agendas also lead to more disagreements among board members. Board members should be required to disclose any potential conflict—business or otherwise—and sign conflict-of-interest and disclosure statements.

13. *Uncontrollable executives.* Executives should receive directions from the board. When the executives make their own strategic choices without recourse to the board, it is a sign that the board has abdicated its responsibility and that the executives have preempted that role. In some cases, a CEO may overstep their position and try to dominate the board by force of personality or charisma.

14. *Micromanagement.* Directors are supposed to make strategic decisions that will lead a company on a solid growth path.

If directors get bogged down in trying to micromanage the executives, they are likely to lose their strategic vision, putting the company's future at risk. This happens where there are no firm guidelines about where board oversight leaves off, and executive management begins. Executive directors may find themselves making statements such as "The board questions everything I do," "I can't even order stationery without the board wanting to get involved," "The board chair doesn't recognize my authority," or "If the board chair doesn't stop sending me those nasty emails I'm going to quit!"

15. *Domineering or disruptive members.* Members of a board of directors should work as a team. The board's ability to make the best decision is compromised when one or two directors dominate meetings. This may involve disruptive behaviors, such as harassment of other directors, talking loudly to dominate the conversation, causing friction, exhibiting a lack of cooperation, or shooting down any dissenting opinions.

16. *Weak or lack of participation.* Some directors sit on a board only for prestige and remain submissive onlookers. These members may attend meetings but rarely speak or offer any opinions on decisions. A lack of participation means that there will be inadequate debates and few overt disagreements or differences of opinion. Submissive onlookers put the company at risk and may be more damaging than those members who are domineering.

17. *No external advisers.* While directors are generally intelligent people, they cannot know everything and should periodically rely on external advisers. A complete lack of technical advisers may indicate a collective arrogance that can lead a company astray. The effect of a lack of technical advisers can become more apparent during a crisis.

18. *Irregular meeting attendance.* Regular meeting attendance is considered a symbol of the committed board and individual director. The most productive board member is the member that is always present. Not only is attendance essential to ensure

productivity, but adequate member attendance also ensures a quorum at every meeting. Perpetual absenteeism among members, and the inability to have a quorum, will hinder the board's progress and ability to act on critical issues.

19. *Lack of a practical performance evaluation.* Lack of constructive performance feedback is self-destructive. Behavioral psychologists and organizational learning experts agree that people and organizations cannot learn without feedback. No matter how good a board is, it is bound to improve if it is periodically reviewed and evaluated intelligently.

20. *Lack of independence.* On boards where everyone is related to everyone in one way or the other portends ill for the company. This situation promotes groupthink and reduces the opportunity for objective discussions. Independent directors also help ensure that issues are assessed openly and objectively, bring an unbiased view to board deliberations, and act in the best interest of all stakeholders.

Finally, a well-functioning board can be instrumental in guiding a company to high levels of success. The key, however, is to recognize the signs of dysfunctional conduct among members before they impair the performance of the entire board.

Dysfunctional Characters at the Board Table

Sometimes the board is dysfunctional because of the character traits of individual directors.

The character types described below are from "20 Dysfunctional Board Member Character Types," by Eileen Morgan Johnson, counsel at Whiteford, Taylor & Preston, LLP; and used with permission from the author.[136]

Board Chairs

Dictator — The Chair as Dictator does not believe in seeking advice or input from fellow board members, staff, or consultants because s/he knows what is best for the company and will take action and then (sometimes) report to the board what has been decided or done. Board members are not allowed to express dissenting views and may be rewarded with or stripped of committee assignments or leadership positions depending on the dictator's whim.

King/Queen — The Chair as King or Queen will seek advice or input from fellow board members, staff, or consultants and then make a pronouncement as to what will be done. King/Queen always rules their kingdom by decrees. Discussion among the board is "encouraged" but only up to a point. The remaining members of the board play the role of "counselors in waiting."

Machiavelli — The Chair as Machiavelli is a strategist. You never can tell what the Chair is thinking or planning. S/he will consistently say to each member of the board what they want to hear to gain their cooperation. S/he will occasionally pull the rug out from under members who have signed on as supporters. Board meeting discussions wander and often go nowhere until the Chair pronounces the "result" of the debate. There is usually a power play in the works, with the chair's trusted spies and lieutenants deployed to plant information, secure support, and report back.

Playwright — The Chair as the Playwright scripts out every possible scenario before the board meeting and assigns roles to those selected "players" on the board who can be counted on to play their roles and speak their lines. The Playwright sometimes becomes the Director when board members forget their lines or digress, but s/he is fast on her feet and gets them all back on script. Committee chairs and officers are well-rehearsed before they assume their duties, and they frequently check in with the Playwright to ensure they are sticking to the script.

Directors

CEO Wannabe — The CEO Wannabe is typically an executive director who wants the CEO's job; they take every opportunity to tell the board that the CEO is ineffective. They undercut the CEO with the rest of the board by comments and suggestive remarks that cast doubt about the CEO's capabilities and performance without actually leveling any concrete charges or producing any evidence of poor performance.

Skeptic — The Skeptic doubts any statement made or report received from staff or consultants; they question the mission statement, the vision and values document, the strategic plan, and all programs and budgets— not in a constructive way but with snide comments and cutting remarks. Anything done by a prior board is suspect. The Skeptic will sometimes abstain from critical votes to avoid being on record. Doing so makes it easier for the Skeptic to criticize board decisions later.

Expert — The Expert tells their fellow directors how to do their jobs. They have an opinion on everything and are always the first to speak up and express their views on any subject. They frequently dominate the discussion at board meetings and are quick to dismiss other directors' comments or opinions with a rehash of technical jargon.

Bomber — The Bomber likes to throw a bomb during a board meeting and then sit back and watch what happens, delighting in the confusion that ensures. Their goal is to disrupt not only the meeting but the board itself. Sometimes the reasons for the "bomb" are not apparent, but most likely because the Bomber wants to discredit other directors (most likely the chair or CEO).

White Rabbit — The White Rabbit is always late for board and committee meetings and generally fails to complete assigned tasks. They always seem so busy that their fellow directors assume they must be doing something worthwhile and of value to the company, but no one really knows what that is. The White Rabbit can lead the board down various dead-end paths.

Big Daddy — Big Daddy is so well known in his hometown (or state or region) that he has a somewhat inflated sense of his own importance. He shoots his mouth off whether the comments are pertinent or not and may need to step out of board meetings for important calls. Big Daddy will make sure everyone knows when and why he has to step away. Big Daddy's mobile phone is the most likely to ring during a board meeting, and he is most likely to be speaking to a "powerful" friend. This could also refer to "Big Mummy."

Absentia — Absentia does not make much of an impression on his fellow board members because they are never there. Although they sometimes sign onto conference calls, no one can tell if they have dropped off. They will not give up their board seat, there are no term limits, and they keep getting re-elected for some reason.

Historian — The Historian has been around since the beginning of time and claims to recall every board decision as if it were made yesterday. They are the only members who track all of the unwritten procedures and policies of the company and can frequently be overheard saying, "that's not how we do it," or "we've always done it this way," or "we tried that before, and it didn't work." The Historian can (and will) tell you why every new idea was tried before with disastrous results.

These characters may seem extreme or unfounded, but I have seen and experienced all of them, with varying outcomes.

There are many forms of dysfunctionality within boards, some that can be quickly addressed and others that can be more difficult to resolve. *What can be done to prevent or reduce the likelihood of having a dysfunctional board?* First, the story below provides the impetus for action.

XYZ was a private high-tech company with a multibillion-pound turnover and institutional shareholders. It had seven executive directors, five non-executive directors, a poisonous internal atmosphere, several individuals who could not stand one another, and intense personal rivalries that continued down the departmental hierarchies. This intense rivalry led to weak cooperation between functional departments and strategic business units that the business underperformed.

The chief executive was a capable engineer and strategist, a personable individual who simply had no idea how to manage his team to deal with this friction and inefficiencies. He would encourage his directors to bring proposals to the executive board but then leave them unsupported and allow the "ravening pack" to compete for resources and status.

The non-executive chairman should have played a significant part in resolving the issues of the dysfunctional board but failed to do so. The department heads had established expert power in their roles and were hard to replace. The problems were of a governance nature based on systems, procedures, and behaviors that an organization is managed.

The board was ineffective in the exercise of its responsibilities. They could not provide strategic direction nor perform their oversight function. The negative impact was economically significant, with a reduction in return on equity over time. The eventual outcome was that the shareholders eventually replaced almost the entire board and executive in order to save the company and their investment. So everyone lost.

There are some strategies a company can adopt proactively to improve the behavior of directors and lower the chances of dysfunctionality.

- Determine an optimal competency and behavioral mix for the board.
- "Recruit for character and train for competence." Often boards' approach in nominating board candidates is the other way around—they look for existing competence in specific skills during the nominating process and then try to shape character once the director has been appointed. A director can be highly skilled in a particular competence yet poor in character and behavior. It is possible to train a director in the skills necessary for a board position, but it is almost impossible to train for the character once someone is already on your board.
- Ensure a governance structure that will facilitate behavior and character aspects in the nominating process. This means providing prospective directors, appointing bodies, and nominating committees with clear expectations around boardroom behaviors in addition to specifics about the roles and responsibilities of a director. Adequate due diligence should be done before an appointment.

- Behavior and character indicators should be incorporated in the annual evaluation process. Including questions in the evaluation tool/system regarding boardroom behavior, relationships, and aspects of the character should reveal these problems in the boardroom and provide a mechanism for beginning a dialogue about how to resolve them. A portion of the board's training budget should be spent on soft skills, not just on "hard" structural and process skills.

- Educate prospective and existing directors on the behavioral expectations of directorship. Educating prospective and current directors includes ensuring these elements are included in the directors' TOR (Terms of Reference) and articulated in the board charter. Sadly some boards overlook the importance of having a formal TOR for directors or a board charter.

From Dysfunctionality to Functionality

What are the steps to take in dealing with problem directors when dysfunctionality is full-blown?

Dealing with problem directors can be both challenging and stressful. There are, however, some practical steps that boards can take. The following highlights the main steps:

1. The board can "live with it."

   - Try to ignore bad behavior at meetings. There are times that though the behavior of others may not be entirely appropriate, we simply need to look past the behavior and focus on the work of the board.

   - Wait until terms are up and hope certain directors do not get re-elected/re-appointed. In organizations in which external bodies and shareholders appoint directors, or they are elected, sometimes you "get who you get." Unless the director is having a negative impact on the organization itself, the board may have to make the most of a problematic director or situation until they are no longer on the board.

- Set maximum term limits in bylaws and ride it out. While this is not the optimal approach for dealing with challenging behavioral issues, it is an approach that is commonly cited.
- Set age (retirement) limits. Again, this is not an optimal approach to board renewal but has been used to some effect.
- The approach of "living with it" can work if the problems are minor.

2. The board (led by the chair) can confront it.

- Ensure the chair meets with the director(s) creating the problems.
- Ensure the vice-chair steps up and confronts the chair if he/she is the problem.
- Have other directors pressure the chair to deal with problem directors.
- This approach can work if the director is willing and able to change; if not, more severe steps will need to be taken.

3. The board can embark on a process of remediation.

- Provide training programs (structural and behavioral).
- Provide coaching (individual and/or board).
- Bring in outside help: lawyer, governance expert, experienced board member, etc.
- This approach can work if the director(s) are willing to change but needs to learn how.

4. The board can seek the resignation of the problematic director(s).

- Underperforming or disruptive directors can be asked to resign.

- This can be accomplished either voluntarily (preferably) or under pressure.
- This approach can work if the director is unwilling or unable to change but wishes to preserve their reputation.

5. The board can remove the problem director(s):

- As a last resort, a board may have to remove a director "for cause."
- The board must be able to demonstrate cause:
    o breach of fiduciary duty (conflict of interest, personal gain)
    o breach of duty of care (privacy, confidentiality, lack of due diligence)
- This approach can work if the director is unwilling and unable to change or resign.

6. The board can recruit for the optimal behavior mix.

- Getting the right directors on the front end is better to avoid going through the previously mentioned escalation steps.
- Ensure a board committee takes responsibility for nominations, including those boards that have directors appointed or elected. This should be either the governance committee or a separate nominating committee.
- Get the right people on the nominating committee. Ensure the individuals have the appropriate skills suited to the work of the committee
- Build an excellent foundational structure for the committee, including terms of reference, annual work plans, budget, and agendas.
- Constitute the committee as a standing committee rather than reconfiguring it each year. This way, committee members can better understand the required matrix and develop a pool of prospects. If the committee is reconstituted each year, it tends to rush to find a willing member to run for the board.

- Educate appointing bodies, the electorate, prospective directors, existing directors, on the organization, expectations of directors (including behavioral expectations), and on the needs and strategy of the organization.
- Determine an optimal behavioral mix for your board.
- Use tools to determine the character and behavior of prospective and existing directors.

Quick Check: Question for Boards and Executives

- Does your board have committed directors who can hold one another to account and are focused on results?
- Do you recognize any of the dysfunctional character types described above on your Board?
- What about the signs of dysfunctionality? Do you recognize any of these on your Board?
- Are there clear guidelines about where board oversight leaves off, and executive management begins?
- How do the chairperson and the board typically deal with a problematic director or an issue that portends dysfunctionality?
- Have you had a board evaluation exercise conducted recently, and did any of these issues come up for discussion? How were the problems handled?
- How aware are you of what is happening in the company you are responsible for governing?
- What issues do you see always being discussed by the board but never resolved?
- Is your board spending enough time on the stuff that matters rather than on the things it has to do (or is used to doing)?
- How well do board members know and trust each other?
- How would your board members describe the company's culture? Would they all describe it the same way, and is the culture consistent across the company?

CHAPTER 10

DYNAMICS OF BOARD DIVERSITY

The word *diversity* suggests *differences* or *variety*. Diversity in the boardroom refers to a board that intentionally appoints directors comprised of individuals with different or a combination of attributes. Diversity is essential in the boardroom because it allows for different perspectives and opinions that can impact the company's decision-making process, ultimately affecting the company's performance. Board diversity is justified as a key to better corporate governance.

Given the importance of boards as the key governing body and one of the principal groups to make corporate decisions, many studies have focused on the connection between board effectiveness and different board characteristics, including various aspects of board diversity. The importance of understanding the role of diversity is also recognized by regulators.

This chapter elaborates on the concept of board diversity and how it may benefit the company, followed by a discussion on the possible costs and downsides and the implementation dynamics.

Defining Diversity

Diversity means more than just acknowledging or tolerating differences. Diversity is a set of conscious practices that involve understanding and appreciating the interdependence of humanity, practicing mutual respect for attributes that are different from ours, and building alliances across differences so that people can work together.

Diversity includes, therefore, knowing how to relate to those attributes that are different from our own and outside the groups to which we belong, yet are present in other individuals and groups. Different attributes come to mind when attempting to describe and define diversity, such as:

- Age
- Ethnicity
- Gender
- Skills
- Experience
- Competencies
- Philosophies

- Life experiences
- Political affiliations
- Race
- Culture
- Religion

A 2020 survey by Heidrick & Struggles showed that boards are increasingly looking to add members with diverse skills that can help them steer their companies through current challenges. Regardless of the demographic dimensions of diversity, however, Russell Reynolds & Associates stated in a report[137] that "diversity for its own sake falls short of both the need and the opportunity."

Here is a good summary of board diversity:

'The best boards are composed of individuals with different skills, knowledge, information, power, and time to contribute. Given the diversity of expertise, information, and availability needed to understand and govern today's complex businesses, it is unrealistic to expect an individual director to be knowledgeable and informed about all phases of business. It is also unrealistic to expect individual directors to be available and to influence all decisions. Thus, in staffing most boards, it is best to think of individuals contributing different pieces to the total picture it takes to create an effective board[138].'

Benefits of Board Diversity

As corporate governance and board practices evolve, boards realize that the breadth of perspective, not the mere inclusion of various diverse elements, benefits the company. Several studies have proven that board diversity adds value to the board's performance and ultimately helps the company and its stakeholders. Diversifying the board can broadly have the following benefits:

- *Effective decision making:* It is believed that a diverse board can make decisions more effectively by reducing the risk of 'groupthink.' Groupthink is described as a psychological behavior of minimizing conflicts and reaching a consensus decision without critically evaluating alternative ideas. On the other hand, combining the contributions of a group of people with different skills, backgrounds and experiences help to consider a matter from a broader range of perspectives, debate more vigorously and raise challenging questions. Having multiple perspectives changes the boardroom dynamics and is more likely to produce higher quality decisions than in a 'groupthink' environment. Also, diversity fosters creativity in delivering solutions to problems and provides more comprehensive oversight of the company's operations. Harvard Business Review found diverse boards can solve problems faster than a board with cognitively similar people.

- *Better stakeholder engagement:* Some companies may benefit more from conforming to societal expectations than others. While shareholders are often the focus of a company's activities, boards need to consider all their stakeholders because they support the processes and activities that support their expectations. Moreover, Companies now compete in a global environment, and to achieve corporate goals and objectives, directors need to understand diverse stakeholders' needs very well. A balanced board will have more representatives of users and customers of its products in the boardroom to make informed decisions. For example, it would be appropriate for multinational companies to include foreign nationals on the board. And for a company that produces cosmetics to have women on the board. Differences in backgrounds, experience, and social networks in the boardroom may enhance the board's understanding of the stakeholders and help address stakeholders' needs more responsively.

- *Overcoming 'director shortage':* One of the problems that boards face in identifying directors for an appointment is 'director shortage.' Searching for directors with a narrow mindset or without a diversity lens is bound to encounter the 'director shortage' brick wall. For most boards, searching for suitable directors, there is a tendency to search for board members with typical characteristics, such as male directors. Suppose boards expand the pool of potential candidates by considering more diversified attributes, like women and ethnic minorities, to be included in the boardroom. In that case, it might alleviate the problem of 'director shortage' and open a broader talent pool. It is therefore vital for companies to tap into the under-utilized pool of talent through board diversity.

- *Reputation enhancement and legitimacy:* Having a heterogeneous board is a way of maintaining a good reputation by establishing the company as a responsible corporate citizen. It signals positively to the internal and external stakeholders that the company emphasizes diverse constituencies and does not discriminate against minorities in climbing the corporate ladder. It is also argued that board diversity reflects the diversity of the society and community served by the company. This reflection strengthens the social contract between a business and its stakeholders, which, in turn, improves the strategic fit that the company has with its environment. For some companies, having a more diverse board can be a means of acquiring legitimacy in the view of the public, the media, and the government.

- *Stronger investor relations:* More institutional investors consider board diversity as a factor for investment evaluation—the reason being that several academic research papers indicated the positive correlation between firm value and board diversity. In addition, institutional investors are placing greater emphasis on corporate social responsibility and believe that board diversity can, to a large extent, improve the corporate social responsibility agenda of a company. Consumer goods companies may want to cultivate a strong image of social responsibility. Also, companies in which institutional investors comprise a significant fraction of their shareholder base may surrender to investors' demand for board diversity. These companies are more likely to pay attention to director demographics, especially gender and ethnicity. In the US, investment companies like BlackRock and State Street are asking companies they invest in to report their board diversity and improve it.

- *A stronger company*: Building a robust and diverse company needs to be supported by diversity at the board level to maximize corporate effectiveness. The board has a responsibility to set the tone at the top that diversity matters. Setting an example at the top on the importance of diversity should have a trickle-down effect within the company, encouraging diversity through the rank and file of the company. Board diversity signals to employees that the company is committed to promoting minority workers or at least that their minority status does not hinder their career progression in the company.

- *Access to resources and connections:* Companies may gain access to different resources by selecting directors with diverse attributes. For example, directors with financial services sector experience can help the company gain access to specific investors or a pool of investors. Directors with political connections may help the company deal with the regulator or win government contracts. Younger directors may help the company engage better with youths or understand emerging technology platforms with which the younger demographics are conversant.

- *Enhanced mentoring and oversight of management:* It has been my experience that improving diversity on the board of an underperforming company can significantly improve its ability to mentor and oversee management. Studies have found that adding directors with different backgrounds, skills, and perspectives helps a board provide management with advice and guidance from a wider variety of perspectives and with respect to more aspects of a company's business. Improving cognitive diversity can enhance a board's ability to perform its oversight functions by increasing the likelihood that management is supervised by knowledgeable and engaged directors who lack a prior relationship with the CEO.

- *A catalyst for change:* Improving diversity in the boardroom increases the likelihood that a board will take steps to address a company's challenges. In my experience, as diversity increases and a board becomes more engaged and professional in its practices, it becomes less likely that important concerns will be ignored by directors or receive scant attention. A director during an interview gave a simple example to illustrate this. *"After the CEO of an underperforming company gave the board an update on the company's performance that indicated that one of its businesses would again be performing more poorly than projected, the incumbent directors remained silent, being accustomed to receiving such news. A newer, cognitively diverse board member broke the silence and asked, "OK, so what do we have to do to improve revenues? What are your plans to address this?"* "It was an obvious question," the director said, "but one that members of the board likely would not have asked in the past." Investors have described how new directors added because of shareholder activism "helped push the board past status quo thinkers" and take steps that many on the board knew were necessary, such as replacing an underperforming CEO or selling a non-core business.

- *Better corporate performance:* All the above benefits will deliver a superior corporate result because a board affects how a company functions and performs. Institutional investors have found that improving diversity on the boards of companies with composition issues can meaningfully enhance board performance. Several studies, including ones by McKinsey & Company, BCG, and Deloitte, have shown a correlation between diverse leadership and a company's financial performance. Stocks for socially responsible companies that abide by specific environmental, social, and corporate governance criteria, including diversity, outperform their peers. "Now that we know diverse boards perform better financially, they have a fiduciary responsibility to diversify," says Stephanie Lampkin, founder and CEO of diversity analytics.

The Gender Diversity Agenda

A standard and straightforward measure to promote heterogeneity in the boardroom includes female representation - commonly known as gender diversity. Gender representation on corporate boards of directors refers to the proportion of men and women who occupy board positions. Studies often use the percentage of women holding corporate board seats and companies with at least one woman on their board to measure gender diversity on corporate boards. Globally, men occupy more board seats than women. Women hold only about a quarter of board seats at the biggest 1,000 companies in the US, according to data from the beginning of 2021 from corporate governance data firm Equilar. While there is slight variation by industry, it is uniformly low.

The representation of women in companies has become an increasingly important topic for academics and practitioners. Today, women account for about 70 percent of the global consumer demand[139] and control about $28 trillion in annual consumer spending.[140] For companies to thrive and grow, corporate boardrooms need to reflect the diversity of their consumer base. Efforts to ensure better representation of women on boards echo the United Nations Sustainable Development Goals (SDGs) proposed in 2015. *Among*

other goals, they affirm the importance of ensuring that women have equal access and participate fully and effectively in leadership roles at all levels of decision-making, whether in political, economic, or public life (SDG 5). F

Despite the growing presence of women in the workforce, representation of women on boards is relatively low. The reason behind the disproportionate gender ratio of directors is a subject of much debate. A survey of more than 4000 directors found that male directors over the age of 55 cited a lack of qualified female candidates as the main reason behind the stagnant number of female directors[141]. In contrast, in the same study, female directors and younger male directors considered the male-dominated networking that often led to the appointment of directors to be the reason behind women's slow progress.

As I write this section, the news broke that there were several female leadership appointments, which caused a ripple in the business environment in Nigeria. In what many observers described as a paradigm shift, the Nigerian banking sector experienced a surge in women at its top echelon. Presently, eight women serve as Chief Executive Officers of the country's leading banks. Despite this impressive status, the Professional Women Roundtable (PWR) Advisory released a report in 2021 on board gender diversity trends in Nigeria's corporate organizations, which indicates that "women hold less than 25 percent corporate board positions in Nigeria." The study was based on the top 20 companies quoted on the Nigerian Exchange (NGX).

Heidrick & Struggles' analysis of 2019 new director appointments in Europe reveals that predominantly female appointees have come from more atypical career backgrounds. For example, seven out of eight board members in FTSE 250 companies with experience as a Chief Human Resources Officer (CHRO) are women. Three out of four board members with experience as a Chief Information Officer (CIO) or Chief Technology Officer (CTO) are women. Five out of six board members with experience as a Chief Marketing Officer (CMO) are women. Considering that less than a third of FTSE 250 board seats in the United Kingdom are occupied by women, these statistics reveal how boards add valuable experience with an increase in female representation.[142]

According to a Board Monitor Europe 2019 report, 38 percent of new board positions in Europe were filled by women during the previous year, an increase over recent years, driven in part by government quotas and the growing realization of the commercial benefit of diversity.[143] As good as these survey outcomes appear, strategies to influence gender diversity in some countries are still evolving. Women in these countries still face discrimination due to stereotyping in certain areas because of outdated thinking and practices.

There are two questions worth considering (1) Do women change boards? (2) Does gender diversity affect a company's outcomes? (3) Why is female representation on boards still low?

1. Do women change boards?
    - *Attendance at board meetings:* In most countries, the Securities and Exchange Commission (SEC) requires listed companies to disclose attendance at board meetings. Therefore, identifying which directors have a poor attendance history in any given year is possible. It has been established that a female director is significantly less likely to be absent from board meetings. Furthermore, male attendance also appears to improve in boards with relatively more female directors. These suggest that the addition of women to boards changes the behavior of all board members. The key lesson from the attendance data is that more women on boards are associated with a more active board.
    - *Board committee composition:* Another way of understanding how women change boards is to see how they are deployed. Board committees such as audit, nominating, corporate governance, and compensation specialize in narrowly defined tasks and are usually considered the important monitoring committees. Studies on board committee composition find that female directors are more likely to be appointed to audit, corporate governance, and nominating

committees than male directors. This suggests that gender-diverse boards allocate more effort to monitoring. Interestingly, female directors are less likely to be assigned to compensation committees than male directors. It is suggested that (male) CEOs' influence on the composition of board committees might be one possible explanation for the relative underrepresentation of women on compensation committees[144].

- *Director compensation structure:* Despite not having a discernible impact on CEO compensation (since female directors are less likely to be assigned to compensation committees), female directors appear to affect director compensation. A study on *Women in the boardroom and their impact on governance and performance*[145] showed that the proportion of overall director compensation paid in stock options and deferred shares is higher in firms with relatively more women on boards. However, there is no apparent impact on the overall level of director pay. Whether equity-based compensation for directors is good or bad depends on one's view of how stock markets work. Stock ownership aligns directors' and shareholders' interests in relatively efficient markets when no significant distinction exists between long-term and short-term shareholders.

2. Does gender diversity affect a company's outcomes?

- *CEO turnover:* An interesting result in the board diversity literature is the impact of board gender diversity on CEO turnover. From a theoretical viewpoint, whether and how diversity should matter for CEO turnover is unclear. However, studies suggest that boards with relatively more female directors are more likely to hold CEOs accountable for poor stock price performance. CEO turnover is more sensitive to stock return performance in companies with relatively more women on boards. A gender-balanced board is more willing to take action after problems are encountered, even if the CEO has to be removed.

- *Market value and operating performance:* No question has attracted more attention in the gender diversity studies than the link between women on boards and the bottom line. Catalyst, a nonprofit organization seeking to promote women in business, regularly produces reports showing correlations between accounting performance and female directors on the boards of Fortune 500 companies. Catalyst reports that companies with a representation of three or more women on their boards significantly outperformed those with low representation by 84 percent on return on sales, by 60 percent on return on invested capital, and by 46 percent on return on equity[146]. In 2016, under my leadership, IFC's Africa Corporate Governance Program, in collaboration with the University of Ghana Business School, conducted a study on women on boards of corporate and public institutions in Ghana. The report, Gender Diversity in Ghanaian Boardrooms, based on the analysis, states that "companies that perform better tend to have more gender-balanced boards. Based on return on assets, high-performing firms were associated with higher gender diversity than low-performing firms." According to a study by McKinsey, gender-diverse companies are 15 percent more likely to have financial returns above their respective national industry medians.[147]

Despite the usual disclaimer that "correlation does not imply causation" that accompanies these reports, the language and the use of the reports implicitly suggest that having more women on boards is a way of improving financial performance.

3. Why is female representation on boards still low?

The representation of women on corporate boards continues to increase, but the number of women leading boards remains low globally[148].

- Women occupy only 19 percent of board seats globally.
- Less than 5 percent of the CEOs of the world's largest corporations are women.
- Only 13 percent of companies surveyed have gender-balanced boards of between 40 and 60 percent women.

All too often, the low representation of women in boardrooms is explained more by socio-cultural factors rather than any organizational flaws or personal issues with these women.

- *Masculine corporate cultures:* The underrepresentation of women on corporate boards can be explained by organizational practices that discriminate against them. The corporate environment is predominantly male, and women have more difficulty accessing positions on the board. In the UK, women working in the financial sector earned 55 percent less annual average gross salaries than their male counterparts[149].

- *Family responsibilities:* An ILO Women in Business and Management report ranks family responsibilities as one of the top barriers to women's leadership. In Asia, 30 percent of business leaders surveyed said many, or most women at mid-career or senior levels who left their jobs, did so voluntarily because of family commitments[150]. Despite anti-discrimination laws in Japan, only 43 percent of women who tried to rejoin the workforce after childbirth found jobs, suggesting a significant cause for a leaky talent pipeline[151].

- *Stereotypes:* Studies show that two-thirds of senior women from corporations and professional firms across Europe highlighted stereotypes and preconceptions of women's roles and abilities as the most critical barrier to their career advancement.[152] Segregation by sex within management functions or the "glass walls" is another barrier to women's leadership. In most companies, a comparatively higher concentration of women is present in specific managerial functions such as human resources, public relations, and communication, and finance and administration in contrast to functions such as operations and sales, research and product management, and general management[153]. This "glass walls" concept makes it difficult for women to sufficiently gather the diverse and broad experiences needed to be selected for top management jobs.

- *Personal barrier:* The personal characteristics of women (skills, abilities, lack of confidence) influence their performance and career success. Research from this perspective suggests that the advancement of women in decision-making positions is more specifically related to their inability to use strategies to cope with all kinds of situations, for example, alliance building, the use of political skills, and the readiness to take risks, etc. The study highlights the importance of training women to overcome certain shortcomings

- *Socio-cultural barriers:* The socio-cultural perspective draws on the weight of tradition and cultural values to explain the low representation of women in the decision-making circle[154]. In Africa, as elsewhere, socio-cultural factors are still frequently mentioned to justify the hierarchy of the sexes. A McKinsey report[155] suggested that the low participation rate of women on boards today can be explained by the renewal of socio-cultural inequities such as (i) the sexual division of labor, (ii) obstacles introduced because of economic constraints including insufficient income, and (iii) institutionalized constraints legitimized by a legal and legislative system that sanctions and renew the subordination of women.

Gender diversity is good for business. Therefore, *boards of the future* must take the gender diversity agenda very seriously.

Possible Costs and Downsides of Board Diversity

Increased globalization and complexity of the business environment have led to the increased necessity for a diverse board. While a diverse board affects the boardroom positively in several ways, there are also some negative impacts of diversity. A company that expects to compete and succeed in the future world order needs to have a balanced perspective and consider the benefits and downsides of diversity in the boardroom.

From a practical perspective, if companies want to choose the composition of their boards to maximize corporate value, they should have at least a qualitative idea about the trade-offs of demographic diversity.

Here are some of the downsides of board diversity that I have come across in my work with boards.

- *Transitioning tension:* For a board that is just beginning to recognize the importance of diversity, there will likely be challenges to creating a more diverse boardroom engagement. Old ways of thinking and entrenched prejudices may hinder the efforts and create tension and conflict. Additionally, as personalities and individual attributes collide, there may be misinterpretations of issues. There is, therefore, a need to ensure buy-in and the willingness to make personal sacrifices in engagement to smoothen transitioning tensions if board diversity is to have its first measure of success.

- *Conflict, lack of cooperation, and insufficient communication.* The social psychology literature provides evidence on the relationship between demographic similarity and attraction. Management studies have developed the concept of group faultlines as *hypothetical dividing lines that may split a group into subgroups based on one or more attributes*[156]. Salient demographic characteristics may split groups into implicit subgroups. Demographic dissimilarity may limit communication among subgroups, create conflict and reduce interpersonal attraction and group cohesiveness. In the case of corporate boards, perhaps a fundamental problem associated with diversity is the possibility of communication breakdown between top executives and minority outside directors. Outside directors rely on executives to gain access to corporate information. Executives may perceive demographically dissimilar directors as sharing different values and espousing different views. The reluctance of executives to share information with minority outside directors could compromise board effectiveness.

- *Real or perceived tokenism:* Another danger of board diversity is sometimes referred to as tokenism. Tokenism is the practice of making only a perfunctory or symbolic effort to do a particular thing, such as recruiting a small number of people from under-represented groups to give the appearance of diversity. Theoretically, the minorities in the boardroom are said to contribute to the value creation of the board by their unique skills and experiences; however, in practice, they may feel that their presence is only to make up the numbers required by the external stakeholders. They may then tend to undervalue their own skills, achievements, and experiences, which demeans their potential contribution to the board and ultimately to the company. Further, the board may potentially ignore the important underlying attributes of successful directors as a sacrifice to meet the requirement of board diversity.

- *Choosing directors with little experience, inadequate qualifications, or who are 'over boarded:* An indirect cost of choosing directors, mainly for their demographic attributes, is a possibility of neglecting other vital characteristics. For example, in the case of gender diversity, because the proportion of women in top executive positions is still small (but growing rapidly), a preference for female directors may lead the board to a female director with relatively little experience. Furthermore, because these qualified minority candidates may be in short supply, minority directors will likely accumulate more board seats than the average director, earning the unenviable status of over-boarded directors. Busy directors are possibly less effective than non-busy ones.

- *Board diversity management:* Board diversity management can help reduce the adverse effects and capitalize on the positive impact of board diversity to enhance board performance. The chairperson's capacity to manage a diverse board is another challenge faced by boards striving to strengthen diversity. Managing diversity is more than simply acknowledging differences in people. The chairperson must be able to coordinate the group and derive value from the combination of diverse attributes. The boardroom environment should also accommodate and be supportive of dissenting viewpoints.

These downsides of board diversity notwithstanding, boards worldwide are making moves to diversify, and regulators are pushing for compliance with board diversity requirements. The board needs to pay special attention to these downsides when implementing measures to diversify the board. It has been proven that board diversity is worth the effort and the investment and that the results are both morally and financially rewarding for the board and the company.

Implementing Board Diversity

Several methods can promote board diversity. Measures currently adopted by different regulatory bodies are generally classified into the following approaches: (i) imposing quotas on the board; and (ii) enhancing disclosures using the 'comply or explain' approach.

Imposing quotas refers to the mandatory requirement in appointing a minimum number of directors with different attributes on the board. This legislation enactment mainly deals with gender diversity to tackle the relative underrepresentation of women in the boardroom. The quota approach has been widely debated in recent years and has met with a fair share of criticism and resistance.

Since 2008, each listed company in Norway has had to ensure that women fill at least 40 percent of directorship positions. A study in 2012 found that while mandatory quotas in Norway increased the representation of women on boards, they also imposed significant and costly constraints on Norwegian companies. Spain, France, and Germany have set gender quotas in the boardroom and made it mandatory for some of Europe's most prominent companies to give women at least 30 percent of board seats.[157] Some African countries adopted the quota agenda in a variety of ways. For example, in Nigeria, it was only mandated for the banking sector.

Supporters of quotas argue that legislated boardroom quotas are essential to gain sufficient momentum to increase boardroom diversity. The quotas are expected to help achieve long-term positive effects by slowly changing perceptions and providing mentors and role models to potential women leaders.

Quota critics note that legislated quotas may inadvertently stigmatize women as their board appointments may be perceived as "tokenistic."[158] As described above, tokenism is the practice of making only a perfunctory or symbolic effort to do a particular thing to give the appearance of compliance. When companies resort to making superficial attempts to include underrepresented groups to tick a box, the problem begins in the diversity implementation effort. To prevent actual or perceived tokenism, concerted efforts must be made to increase the number of the underrepresented group and create an environment that recognizes their input.

An alternate approach to legislated quotas is setting voluntary targets by companies to advocate an increase in women's representation on boards. In 2011, the Lord Davies report recommended against adopting mandatory quotas in the UK and argued that voluntary targets should be set and "board appointments should be made based on business needs, skills, and ability."[159] The voluntary approach in the UK yielded positive results as the representation of women on boards increased to 23.5 percent within a short timeframe[160]. Deutsche Telekom, a leading German telecommunications company, recorded a success. It had set a voluntary quota in 2010 to increase women's representation on its board. Within five years, the company successfully achieved 40 percent women on its group supervisory board[161].

However, many companies have not made appreciable progress despite voluntary efforts. For example, in the US, women's representation on boards only increased to 17 percent despite significant efforts by companies.[162] The question of whether to adopt mandatory quotas or voluntary targets remains a controversial one, but certainly, the discourse is raising awareness.

Another measure to enhance board diversity is through transparency and disclosure. Under some corporate governance codes, companies must disclose their diversity policy in appointing directors so that investors and stakeholders can make informed decisions. Those who fail to implement such measures must explain their non-compliance in the corporate governance report or equivalent.

The UK Corporate Governance Code, for example, stipulates that companies are required to incorporate diversity as a consideration in making board appointments; and disclose in their annual reports describing the board's policy on diversity, as well as its progress in achieving the objectives of that policy. Australia and Hong Kong are promoting diversity using a similar 'comply or explain' approach. South Africa and Nigeria are using the 'comply and explain' approach to achieve the same result.

In implementing policies on board diversity, both the board chairperson and the nomination committee play significant roles. Being the board leader, the chairperson has to facilitate new directors joining the board and encourage open discussions and exchanges of information during formal and informal meetings. To create such a well-functioning board, the chairperson needs to commit and support mentoring, networking, and adequate training for board members.

The nomination committee should consider diversity and establish a formal recruitment policy concerning the variety of competencies required for the board, its business nature, and its strategies. The committee members must carefully analyze what the board lacks in skills and expertise and advertise board positions periodically. They are strongly encouraged not to seek candidates merely through personal contacts and networks but to carry out a formal and transparent nomination process.

The board recruitment and evaluation process should be dynamic, recognizing individual skills and capabilities against traditional approaches based mainly on experience, usually in a particular industry. Demographically diverse director candidates should be selected who have strong business backgrounds. As one director stated, *"A director must have the business background and experience to ask intelligent questions and hold management accountable. Then if the director adds diversity of race, gender, or age to the board, it is a plus. Without such experience, it is less likely that a new director will add significant value."*

However, an essential ingredient to the success of board diversity would most probably be the board members changing their mindset to welcome a more heterogeneous board and place greater trust in one another and work together more effectively. Finally, to facilitate the likelihood that new directors express their perspectives during boardroom deliberations, I recommend that boards take formal induction and onboarding seriously and emphasize the importance of participation during the onboarding process.

Among other things, new directors need to be told that the board welcomes directors sharing their thoughts and perspectives when they differ from others in the boardroom and counting on them to do so. The view that new directors should primarily be observers on a board while learning the "lay of the land" is outdated. We also recommend that directors be encouraged to ask questions regarding matters they do not understand or that do not seem clear to them. Often others in the boardroom will benefit from the inquiry.

While it is labor-intensive, diligent director recruiting and onboarding can help ensure that demographically diverse directors selected by a board also improve cognitive diversity and board performance. In the end, the board's goal should be to recruit directors who bring different insights, views, and perspectives and help improve the board's effectiveness.

In summary, there is enormous moral and financial pressure on companies right now to diversify their boards. This pressure will continue for the foreseeable future. One of the central arguments cited for improving the diversity of demographic characteristics on corporate boards is that it is necessary to ensure that boards perform their obligations effectively in today's competitive business landscape. Some companies are making progress, but it might take more systematic change before more diverse, inclusive corporate boards become the norm. If a board is genuinely committed to effectively fulfilling its role and responsibilities, improving board diversity must be prioritized. The future will reward those who make the transition speedily.

Quick Check: Question for Boards and Executives

- How much diversity is there on the board and in the executive team?
- Does your board have the breadth of perspective to address the market landscape that will define your business in the future?
- Does your board value differences in views and perspectives?
- Does the Board understand their own inherent biases and stereotypes, or do they even want to know?
- What are the board's major strengths and areas for improvement?
- What five qualities are essential in new board members?
- Is there a formal process of recruiting new board members that incorporates diversity factors?
- Can your company's reputation be negatively (or positively) impacted by our board's current composition vis-à-vis diversity?
- If someone were to make assumptions about your corporate values based on your board composition, what would they be likely to think?
- Does the organization have diversity included in its succession planning to recruit and retain diverse talent for years to come successfully?

CONCLUSION

Writing this book has been very fulfilling because sharing my proprietary Five-Way-Directional Model© with the corporate world is something that I have wanted to do for a long time. Writing this book was also an opportunity to share from my decades of experience working with boards, board committees, and executive management teams as a coach, advisor, evaluator, trainer, and consultant.

As great as the Five-Way-Directional Model©, I must sound a word of caution that it is not a panacea for all board ailments. It is a pathway or part of a network of pathways to becoming an effective board. The model provides guidance for boards to develop the collective vision and the behaviors it wishes to promote in conducting its business.

Boards need to move from cognitive awareness (of some of these pertinent issues) to committed action (toward addressing the issues noted). Václav Havel, who served as the last president of Czechoslovakia and the first president of the Czech Republic, said, "Vision is not enough; it must be combined with venture. It is not enough to stare up the steps; we must step up the stairs." Stepping up the stairs is what this book challenges directors and the board as a whole to do. Therefore, it offers a valuable tool for those who want to improve their board leadership experience and make a difference in the corporate world.

The Business Landscape Continues to Evolve

The role of companies is evolving in response to the broader patterns of an ever-evolving society, which is continuously shaped by newer generations and their beliefs and behaviors. Future boards need to understand the importance of the long-term factors that will shape performance in the eyes of modern shareholders. Boards need to embrace these changes and develop the ability to flex and adapt to stay fit for purpose.

A 2020 Heidrick & Struggles survey asked how boards will change over the next five years. The overwhelming response was that the board would need to assume a more active role in several corporate activities and spend more time on its responsibilities. The business landscape will continue to evolve.[163]

In addition to many social factors, the current state of the business landscape has given rise to new terminologies, practices, and protocols in the boardroom that may have existed previously but have become more prevalent now. Employee matters have been heightened; digitalization has taken on a new level of importance, including remote technologies for board interactions. Boards of directors are set to take a more active leadership within companies than they have done in the past.

Boards of the future will need to be more diverse in their composition and how they think and act. As one director said, "Boards will be required to find a way to encourage diversity of views and complementary skills, rather than defaulting to easy-to-measure director profiles such as ethnicity [and] gender."

An Ongoing Conversation

The board improvement conversation inspired by the Five-Way-Directional Model© is ongoing; this book is the starting point. And as the business landscape continues to evolve, the discussion will continue to advance in scope and impact.

This book contains much of what current and aspiring board members need to increase their board leadership effectiveness. In addition to the five chapters dedicated to each of the five leadership directions, some topical issues facing boards today and in the future were covered. These topical issues include how the board can navigate crisis and digitalization better by using the Five-Way-Directional Model©. I also addressed the dysfunctionality of boards and how this can be alleviated. Each chapter ends with "Quick Checks: Questions for Boards and Executives," which I included to encourage readers to reflect on the concepts and reinforce the lessons.

As boards adopt the Five-Way-Directional Model©, they will experience clarity by looking through the five lenses. They will find it progressively easy to focus their attention on each direction with intentionality. The model requires directors to look intentionally in each direction, learn from what they see, so that they can lead effectively and, consequently, leap exponentially.

If you are reading this conclusion, you will already know that it is helpful for boards of directors to

1. Look forward strategically, envisioning future business goals and gauging the necessary approaches to achieving the goals.
2. Look backward, retrospectively, contemplating experiences and lessons.
3. Look inward, reflectively, perform a self-directed assessment, and take specific actions based on the assessment outcomes.
4. Look outward, collaboratively, becoming stakeholder-centric.
5. Look upward soberly and discharge their (personal and collective) responsibility ethically, enabling the company to be a good corporate citizen in words and deeds.

Boards that intend to be relevant in the future business landscape will need to develop the skillset and mindset required for effective board work. I invite you to embrace the concepts shared in this book, *Boards of the Future*, as they will remain relevant and continue to promote effectiveness in boardrooms for years ahead.

I hope you found this book an insightful and interesting read and wish you well as you and your board embark on the journey into the future.

REFERENCES

1   World Health Organization. Coronavirus Disease 2019 (COVID-19): Situation Report 100. Geneva (2020).

2   OECD (2015), G20/OECD Principles of Corporate Governance, OECD Publishing, Paris. http://dx.doi.org/10.1787/9789264236882-en. Pg 45

3   Pletzer, J. L., Nikolova, R., Kedzior, K. K., & Voelpel, S. C. (2015). Does gender matter? Female representation on corporate boards and firm financial performance-A meta-analysis. PloS one, 10(6), e0130005.

4   Salmon, Walter J. "Crisis prevention: how to gear up your board." Harvard Business Review 71, no. 1 (1993): 68-75.

5   George, William. "Board governance depends on where you sit." McKinsey Quarterly 1, no. 1 (2013): 80-90.

6   George, William. "Board governance depends on where you sit." McKinsey Quarterly 1, no. 1 (2013): 80-90.

7   https://www.mckinsey.com/business-functions/strategy-and-corporate-finance/our-insights/how-boards-have-risen-to-the-covid-19-challenge-and-whats-next

8   John Strawson, If by Chance: Military Turning Points that Changed History, London: Macmillan, 2003.

9   Heidrick & Struggles International, Inc. 2020, Board of the Future. https://www.heidrick.com/en/insights/boards-governance/board of the future moving toward a more diverse more in tune european board

10 OECD (2015), G20/OECD Principles of Corporate Governance, OECD Publishing, Paris. http://dx.doi.org/10.1787/9789264236882-en. Pg 54

11 Lorsch, Jay William. The future of boards: Meeting the governance challenges of the twenty-first century. Harvard Business Press, 2012.

12 Ibid.

13 OECD, Principles of Corporate Governance (Paris: OECD, 2004), p.24. Available at: http://www.oecd.org/dataoecd/32/18/31557724.pdf .

14 Schmidt, Sascha L., and Matthias Brauer. "Strategic governance: How to assess board effectiveness in guiding strategy execution." Corporate Governance: An International Review 14, no. 1 (2006): 13-22.

15 CECP Board of Boards, Executive Report (2016) http://cecp.co/wp-content/uploads/2016/11/BofB16_Executive_Summary_FINAL_Web.pdf

16 Bhagat, Chinta, Martin Hirt, and Conor Kehoe. "Tapping the strategic potential of boards." (2013).

17 Sonnenfeld, Jeffrey A. "What makes great boards great." Harvard business review 80, no. 9 (2002): 106-113.

18 Casal, Christian, and Christian Caspar. "Building a forward-looking board." McKinsey Quarterly 2 (2014): 119-126.

19 Saylor Academy (2012) https://saylordotorg.github.io/text_corporate-governance/s09-the-board-s-role-in-strategy-d.html (23/06/21)

20 Bhagat, Chinta, Martin Hirt, and Conor Kehoe. "Tapping the strategic potential of boards." (2013).

21 Palepu, Krishna. "Focusing on strategy to govern effectively." JW Lorsch (2012).

22 Krishna Palepu and Jonathan Barnett, "Hewlett-Packard-Compaq: The Merger Decision," Case 104-048 (Boston: Harvard Business School, 2004).

23 Jay Lorsch, Krishna Palepu, Elliott Sherman, and Carin-Isabel Knoop, "Hewlett-Packard Co.: The War Within," Case 107-030 (Boston: Harvard Business School, 2006).

24 Jay Lorsch, Krishna Palepu, and Melissa Barton, "Hewlett-Packard Company: CEO Succession in 2010," Case 411-056 (Boston: Harvard Business School, 2010).

25 Nadler, David A. "Building better boards." *Harvard business review* 82, no. 5 (2004): 102-105.

26 Buiter, W.H., 2007. Lessons from the 2007 financial crisis. *Paper presented at the 25th anniversary Workshop "The Global Financial Crisis: Lessons and Outlook" of the Advanced Studies Program of the IFW, Kiel

on May 8/9, 2009. It develops ideas first discussed in my Den Uyl Lecture (Buiter (2008)),

27 https://hbr.org/2007/09/why-dont-we-learn-from-history-1

28 Paine, Lynn S., and Suraj Srinivasan. "A guide to the big ideas and debates in corporate governance." Harvard Business Review (2019).

29 Hamilton, Stewart, Micklethwait, Alicia. Greed and Corporate Failure – The Lessons from Recent Disasters. Palgrave MacMillian, 2006. 207p.

30 Da Silveira, Alexandre Di Miceli, Corporate Scandals of the 21ˢᵗ Century: Limitations of Mainstream Corporate Governance Literature and the Need for a New Behavioral Approach (November 15, 2015). Available at SSRN: https://ssrn.com/abstract=2181705 or http://dx.doi.org/10.2139/ssrn.2181705

31 https://trainingindustry.com/articles/leadership/why-looking-back-can-help-you-lead-forward/

32 https://en.wikipedia.org/wiki/William_Bridges_(author)

33 Bhagat, Chinta, and Conor Kehoe. "High-performing boards: What's on their agenda?." McKinsey Quarterly (2014).

34 Charan, Ram. Boards that deliver: Advancing corporate governance from compliance to competitive advantage. Vol. 20. John Wiley & Sons, 2011. Page 61

35 Charan, Ram. Boards that deliver: Advancing corporate governance from compliance to competitive advantage. Vol. 20. John Wiley & Sons, 2011. Page 139

36 https://ram-charan.com/

37 Henry Bosch, The Director at Risk (Melborne: Pitman, 1995), p. 142.

38 "The Combined Code" (London: Financial Reporting Council, 2006), p.9. Available at: www.ecgi.org/codes/all_codes.php.

39 Dunning, D., Johnson, K., Ehrlinger, J. and Kruger, J., 2003. Why people fail to recognize their own incompetence. Current directions in psychological science, 12(3), pp.83-87.

40 https://assets.ey.com/content/dam/ey-sites/ey-com/en_us/topics/cbm/ey-how-companies-are-evolving-board-evaluations-and-disclosures.pdf

41 Walton, Anna Elise Elise. "Leveraging board assessment for sustained performance." International Finance Corporations's Private Sector Opinion 33 (2014).

42 Simon Osborne, "Board Performance Evaluation," Private Sector Opinion, Issue 9 (Washington, D.C.: Global Corporate Governance Forum, June 10, 2008).

43 Institute of Chartered Secretaries and Administrators, ICSA Board Evaluation: Review of the UK top 200 companies 2010 (London: ICSA, April 2011), www. icsaglobal.com.

44 Nicholson G, Kiel G and Tunny JA, Forthcoming, 'Board evaluations: Contemporary thinking and practice', in Branson DM and Clarke T (eds), The Sage Handbook of Corporate Governance, London: SAGE Publications Inc

45 Sir Adrian Cadbury in Corporate Governance and Development, Global Corporate Governance Forum, World Bank, 2003.

46 IFC board leadership toolkit, 2007.

47 Preston, Lee E., and Harry J. Sapienza. "Stakeholder management and corporate performance." Journal of behavioral Economics 19, no. 4 (1990): 361-375.

48 Zollinger, P. "Stakeholder Engagement and the Board: Integrating Best Governance Practices, Global Corporate Governance Forum." Focus 8 (2009): 1-6.

49 Slaper, Timothy F., and Tanya J. Hall. "The triple bottom line: What is it and how does it work." Indiana business review 86, no. 1 (2011): 4-8.

50 https://en.wikipedia.org/wiki/Triple_bottom_line

51 https://www.forbes.com/sites/jeroenkraaijenbrink/2019/12/10/what-the-3ps-of-the-triple-bottom-line-really-mean/?sh=39ba78135143

52 Prado-Lorenzo, J.M. and Garcia-Sanchez, I.M., 2010. The role of the board of directors in disseminating relevant information on greenhouse gases. Journal of business ethics, 97(3), pp.391-424.

53 https://boardmember.com/directors-adopt-triple-bottom-line/

54 Zollinger, P. "Stakeholder Engagement and the Board: Integrating Best Governance Practices, Global Corporate Governance Forum." Focus 8 (2009): 1-6.

55 Post, James E., and Tanja D. Carroll. "Governance and the stakeholder corporation: new challenges for global business." Transformations in global governance: implications for multinationals and other stakeholders (2006): 120-145.

56 Post, James E., Lee E. Preston, and Sybille Sauter-Sachs. Redefining the corporation: Stakeholder management and organizational wealth. Stanford University Press, 2002. Page 47

57 Finkelstein, Sydney. Why smart executives fail: And what you can learn from their mistakes. Penguin, 2004.

58 Hemphill, T. (2006). "Corporate Internal Investigations: Balancing Firm Social Reputation with Board Fiduciary Responsibility." Corporate Governance, 6(5), 635-642.

59 https://governanceevaluator.com/resources/stakeholder-engagement-still-a-concern-for-many-boards/

60 Owen, D.L., Swift, T., & Hunt, K. (2001), Questioning the role of stakeholder engagement in social and ethical accounting, auditing and reporting, Accounting Forum, Vol. 25 pp.265.

61 Business Roundtable, "Business roundtable redefines the purpose of a corporation to promote 'an economy that serves all Americans,'" August 19, 2019, businessroundtable.org.

62 https://www.odgersberndtson.com/media/8031/odgers-berndtson-building-a-board-to-face-the-future-thought-paper.pdf

63 https://about.vanguard.com/investment-stewardship/perspectives-and-commentary/what_how_why.pdf.

64 Clarken, R.H., 2009. "Moral Intelligence in the Schools". School of Education, Northern Michigan University. PP. 1-7.

65 Osborn, N., 2011. "Moral Intelligence". Team International, 11107 Wurzbach Road. Suite 102. San Antonio. P.1.

66 Beheshtifar, Malikeh, Zhra Esmaeli, and Mahmoud Nekoie Moghadam. "Effect of moral intelligence on leadership." European Journal of Economics, Finance and Administrative Sciences 43, no. 1 (2011): 6-11.

67 Lennick, D. & Keil, F.K., 2005. "Moral Intelligence". Pearson Education, Inc. Prentice Hall. ISBN 0-13-149050-8. PP. 1-7.

68 Thorhauer, Y. & Blachfellner, S., 2009. "Business Intelligence Meets Moral Intelligence". International Review of Information Ethics. 10 (2), P. 1.

69 Borba, Michele. Building moral intelligence: The seven essential virtues that teach kids to do the right thing. John Wiley & Sons, 2002.

70 Lennick, D. & Keil, F.K., 2005. "Moral Intelligence". Pearson Education, Inc. Prentice Hall. ISBN 0-13-149050-8. PP. 1-7.

71 Manallack, S., 2006. "Ethics, success and leadership". Public Relations and Financial Communication. 64 Tennyson St Elwood VIC 3184. P.2

72 Clarken, R.H., 2009. "Moral Intelligence in the Schools". School of Education, Northern Michigan University. PP. 1-7.

73 Batstone, D., 2003. "Saving the Corporate Soul: Combining Corporate Integrity with the Bottom Line". Wharton School Publishing.

74 McGregor, L.T., 2010. "Consumer Moral Leadership" Mount Saint Vincent University. Canada. PP. 3-8.

75 Maxwell, John C. The right to lead: Learning leadership through character and courage. Thomas Nelson, 2010.

76 Djokic, D., & Duh, M. (2016). Corporate Governance Quality in Selected Transition Countries. Managing Global Transitions, 14(4), 335

77 Puspitasari, Devy M., Sotarduga Napitupulu, and Djoko Roespinoedji. "FIT AND PROPER TEST: A DETERMINANT OF GOOD CORPORATE GOVERNANCE BANKING INDUSTRY IN INDONESIA." PalArch's Journal of Archaeology of Egypt/Egyptology 17, no. 10 (2020): 1061-1083.

78 Tomić, Lucia Ana, David Tomašek, and Marko Žunić. "Fit and Proper Assessment of Board Members." InterEULawEast: journal for the international and european law, economics and market integrations 7, no. 2 (2020): 263-288.

79 Yew, Lee Kuan. From third world to first: The Singapore story, 1965-2000. Marshall Cavendish International Asia Pte Ltd, 2012. Page 6

80 Yew, Lee Kuan. From third world to first: The Singapore story, 1965-2000. Marshall Cavendish International Asia Pte Ltd, 2012. Page 72

81 Leong, Ho Khai. "Prime ministerial leadership and policy-making style in Singapore: Lee Kuan Yew and Goh Chok Tong compared." Asian Journal of Political Science 8, no. 1 (2000): 91-123.

82 Bourke, Juliet, and Andrea Espedido. "Why inclusive leaders are good for organizations, and how to become one." Harvard Business Review Digital Articles 1, no. 1 (2019): 2-5.

83 Dunning, D., Johnson, K., Ehrlinger, J. and Kruger, J., 2003. Why people fail to recognize their own incompetence. Current directions in psychological science, 12(3), pp.83-87.

84 Arnold M. Howitt and Herman B. Leonard, "Against desperate peril: High performance in emergency preparation and response," in Deborah E. Gibbons, ed, Communicable Crises: Prevention, Response, and

Recovery in the Global Arena, first edition, Charlotte, NC: Information Age Publishing, 2007.

85 https://www.pwc.com/us/en/services/governance-insights-center/library/annual-corporate-directors-survey.html.

86 Culled from Navigating (page 15)

87 Zhu, Pearl. Digitizing Boardroom: The Multifaceted Aspects of Digital Ready Boards. Vol. 7. BookBaby, 2016.

88 IFC's publication Navigating Through Crises: A Handbook for Boards (2010) prepared as part of IFC's overall crisis-response program, with funding from the Oesterreichische Entwicklungsbank (OeEB) https://www.ifc.org/wps/wcm/connect/region ext content/ifc external corporate site/east+asia+and+the+pacific/resources/navigating+through+crises+-a+handbook+for+boards.

89 Bennett, Nathan, and James Lemoine. "What VUCA really means for you." Harvard business review 92, no. 1/2 (2014).

90 Arnold Howitt and Herman B. Leonard, eds, Managing Crises: Responses to Large-Scale Emergencies, first edition, Washington, DC: CQ Press, 2009.

91 Nahman Alon and Haim Omer, "The continuity principle: A unified approach to disaster and trauma," American Journal of Community Psychology, 1994, Volume 22, Number 2, pp. 273–87.

92 Bennett, Nathan, and G. James Lemoine. "What a difference a word makes: Understanding threats to performance in a VUCA world." Business Horizons 57, no. 3 (2014): 311-317.

93 IFC's publication Navigating Through Crises: A Handbook for Boards (2010) prepared as part of IFC's overall crisis-response program, with funding from the Oesterreichische Entwicklungsbank (OeEB) Page 60 https://www.ifc.org/wps/wcm/connect/region ext content/ifc external corporate site/east+asia+and+the+pacific/resources/navigating+through+crises+-a+handbook+for+boards

94 D'Auria, Gemma, and Aaron De Smet. "Leadership in a crisis: Responding to the coronavirus outbreak and future challenges." (2020).

95 Amy C. Edmondson, "Don't hide bad news in times of crisis", Harvard Business Review, March 6, 2020, hbr.org.

96 Bennett, Nathan, and G. James Lemoine. "What a difference a word makes: Understanding threats to performance in a VUCA world." Business Horizons 57, no. 3 (2014): 311-317.

97 IFC's publication Navigating Through Crises: A Handbook for Boards (2010) prepared as part of IFC's overall crisis-response program, with funding from the Oesterreichische Entwicklungsbank (OeEB) Page 10 https://www.ifc.org/wps/wcm/connect/region ext content/ ifc external corporate site/east+asia+and+the+pacific/resources/ navigating+through+crises+-a+handbook+for+boards.

98 ibid.

99 https://papers.ssrn.com/sol3/papers.cfm?abstract_id=3363002

100 https://www.ifc.org/wps/wcm/connect/topics_ext_content/ifc_ external_corporate_site/ifc+cg/resources/guidelines_reviews+and+case+ studies/tip+sheet+for+company+leadership+on+crisis+response+-+facing+ the+covid-19+pandemic

101 Bankewitz, Max, Carl Aberg, and Christine Teuchert. "Digitalization and boards of directors: A new era of corporate governance." Business and Management Research 5, no. 2 (2016): 58-69.

102 Heidrick & Struggles International, Inc. 2020, Board of the Future. https://www.heidrick.com/en/insights/boardsgovernance/board_of_the_ future_moving_toward_a_more_diverse_more_in_tune_european_ board

103 Grove, Hugh, Mac Clouse, and Laura Georg Schaffner. "Digitalization impacts on corporate governance." Journal of governance & regulation 7, Iss. 4 (2018): 51-63.

104 Bankewitz, Max, Carl Aberg, and Christine Teuchert. "Digitalization and boards of directors: a new era of corporate governance." Business and Management Research 5, no. 2 (2016): 58-69.

105 Korn/Ferry Institute (2013. "The Digital Board: Appointing Non-Executive Directors for the Internet Economy," Report, London.

106 Gartner Glossary: Digitalization. Available from: www.gartner.com [Accessed 18 June 2021]

107 KPMG 2020 CEO Outlook: COVID-19 Special Edition [Accessed 24 October 2021]

108 https://www.iot-now.com/2020/07/23/104031-covid-19-has-sped-up-digital-transformation-by-5-3-years-says-study/ [Accessed 24 October 2021]

109 World Economic Forum, https://www.weforum.org/centre-for-the-fourth-industrial-revolution/areas-of-focus

110 Lewis-Kraus, G. (2016). "The Great A.I. Awakening," The New York Times, December 14.

111 Walport, M. (2016), "Distribute Ledger Technology: Beyond Block Chain", A Report by the UK Government Chief Scientific Advisor, Open Government License, pp. 1-88.

112 Wiatt, R. (2016). "Manufacturing Enters the Third Dimension," Strategic Finance, December 1.

113 Ng, J. (2016). "The Internet of Things is Already Here. Are You Ready For it?" American Institute of CPAs Communications, June 16.

114 Lev, B. and F. Gu (2016). The End of Accounting and the Path Forward for Investors and Managers, John Wiley & Sons, Inc., Hoboken, New Jersey.

115 Frigo, M. (2012). "The Balanced Scorecard: 20 Years and Counting," Strategic Finance, October, Volume 94, Issue 4, pp. 49-53.

116 Müller, Roland: Digitalization Decisions at the Board Level. In Hilb, Michael (ed.): Governance of Digitalization : The Role of Boards of Directors and Top Management Teams in Digital Value Creation. Bern : Haupt Verlag, 2017, S. 43-50.

117 Valentine, E.L. and Stewart, G., 2013. The emerging role of the board of directors in enterprise business technology governance. International Journal of Disclosure and Governance, 10(4), pp.346-362.

118 Brummer, Chris. Soft law and the global financial system: rule making in the 21st century. Cambridge University Press, 2015.

119 Sarrazin, H. and P. Willmott (2016). "Adapting Your Board to the Digital Age," McKinsey Quarterly, July, pp. 1-10.

120 Celia Huber, Alex Sukharevsky, and Rodney Zemmel (2021) 5 Questions Boards Should Be Asking About Digital Transformation. https://hbr. org/2021/06/5-questions-boards-should-be-asking-about-digital-transformation (21 June 2021)

121 Diana Wu David and Sunshine Farzan, Boards Are Undergoing Their Own Digital Transformation. Harvard Business Review. July 09, 2021

122 Heidrick & Struggles, Board Monitor Europe 2019, September 25, 2019, heidrick.com.

123 Diana Wu David and Sunshine Farzan, Boards Are Undergoing Their Own Digital Transformation. Harvard Business Review. July 09, 2021

124 Diana Wu David and Sunshine Farzan, Boards Are Undergoing Their Own Digital Transformation. Harvard Business Review. July 09, 2021

125 Georg L. (2016). "Information Security Governance: Pending Legal Responsibility of Non-Executive Boards," Journal of Management and Governance, Springer Online, pp. 1-22.

126 Ng, J. (2016). "The Internet of Things is Already Here. Are You Ready For it?" American Institute of CPAs Communications, June 16.

127 Castelluccio, M. (2017). "The Most Notorious Hacks of 2016," Strategic Finance, January 11.

128 Georg L. (2016). "Information Security Governance: Pending Legal Responsibility of Non-Executive Boards," Journal of Management and Governance, Springer Online, pp. 1-22.

129 Celia Huber, Alex Sukharevsky, and Rodney Zemmel (2021) 5 Questions Boards Should Be Asking About Digital Transformation. https://hbr.org/2021/06/5-questions-boards-should-be-asking-about-digital-transformation (21 June 2021)

130 Pande, Aditya, and Christoph Schrey. "Five questions boards should ask about IT in a digital world." McKinsey Online [Online], available at: www. mckinsey. com/business-functions (2016). https://www.mckinsey.com/business-functions/mckinsey-digital/our-insights/five-questions-boards-should-ask-about-it-in-a-digital-world (21 June 2021)

131 Lorsch, Jay William. The future of boards: Meeting the governance challenges of the twenty-first century. Harvard Business Press, 2012.

132 Stanley, Dick. "What do we know about social cohesion: The research perspective of the federal government's social cohesion research network." Canadian Journal of Sociology/Cahiers canadiens de sociologie (2003): 5-17.

133 Zhu, Pearl. Digitizing Boardroom: The Multifaceted Aspects of Digital Ready Boards. Vol. 7. BookBaby, 2016.

134 Arbouw, John. "Measuring boardroom performance." Company Director 14, no. 1 (1998).

135 https://www.samanthamcgolrick.com/blog-31-how-to-create-psychological-safety-at-work-in-the-boardroom/

136 https://nonprofitrisk.org/resources/articles/dysfunctional-characters-often-sit-at-the-board-table/ (23/06/21)

137 https://www.russellreynolds.com/insights/thought-leadership/different-is-better-why-diversity-matters-in-the-boardroom

138 Conger, Jay A., and Edward III Lawler. "Building a high-performing board: How to choose the right members." Business Strategy Review 12, no. 3 (2001): 11-11.

139 Tyson, L. (2015). Promoting gender parity in the global workplace. McKinsey & Company Insights and Publications. [online] Available at: http://www.mckinsey.com/insights/organization/promoting_gender_parity_in_the_global_workplace [Accessed 7 Apr. 2021].

140 Silverstein, M. and Sayre, K. (2009). The Female Economy. Harvard Business Review. [online] Available at: https://hbr.org/2009/09/the-female-economy [Accessed 7 Apr. 2021].

141 Groysberg, Boris; Cheng, Yo-Jud; Stuart, Spencer; Bell, Deborah; The WomenCorporateDirectors Foundation. 2016 Global Board Survey. Retrieved 19 May 2016.

142 Heidrick & Struggles, "Meeting the demand for women directors," December 5, 2018, heidrick.com

143 Heidrick & Struggles, Board Monitor Europe 2019, September 25, 2019, heidrick.com.

144 Ferreira, Daniel. "Board diversity." Corporate governance: A synthesis of theory, research, and practice 8 (2010): 225.

145 Adams, Renee, and Daniel Ferreira. 2009. Women in the boardroom and their impact on governance and performance. Journal of Financial Economics 94 (2): 291–309.

146 Catalyst, (2011). The Bottom Line: Corporate Performance and Women's Representation on Boards (2004-2008).

147 Hunt, V., Layton, D. and Prince, S. (2015). Why diversity matters. McKinsey & Company Insights and Publications. [online] Available at: http://www.mckinsey.com/insights/organization/why_diversity_matters

148 International Labour Organization, (2015). Women in Business and Management: Gaining Momentum Global Report. Geneva

149 Opportunity Now, (n.d.). International Women's Day Factsheet - Women and Work (UK)

150 McKinsey & Company, (2012). Women Matter – An Asian Perspective

151 Harvard Business Review staff, (2013). Women and the economics of equality. Harvard Business Review

152 European Commission, (2010). More women in senior positions: Key to economic stability and growth

153 International Labour Organization, (2015). Women in Business and Management: Gaining Momentum Global Report. Geneva

154 Letza, S. (2017). Corporate governance and the African business context: the case of Nigeria. Economics and Business Review, 3(17), No. 1, 2017, 184-204

155 McKinsey. (2016). Women matter Africa. Pretoria, Annual Report.

156 Ferreira, Daniel. "Board diversity." Corporate governance: A synthesis of theory, research, and practice 8 (2010): 225.

157 Smale, A. and Cain Miller, C. (2015). Germany Sets Gender Quotas in Boardrooms. The New York Times. [online] Available at: http://www. nytimes.com/2015/03/07/world/europe/german-law-requires-more-women-oncorporate-boards.html? r=0

158 Lukas, C. (2014). Boardroom Quotas Won't Help Women. The New York Times. [online] Available at: http://www.nytimes.com/2014/12/08/opinion/boardroom-quotas-wont-help-women.html

159 Lord Davies of Abersoch, (2011). The Davies Report 'Women on Boards', United Kingdom

160 Hope, K. (2015). FTSE 100 firms appoint more women to their boards. BBC News. [online] Available at: http://www.bbc.com/news/business-32038561

161 Smale, A. and Cain Miller, C. (2015). Germany Sets Gender Quotas in Boardrooms. The New York Times. [online] Available at: http://www. nytimes.com/2015/03/07/world/europe/german-law-requires-more-women-oncorporate-boards.html? r=0

162 Bernard, T. (2014). Vigilant Eye on Gender Pay Gap. The New York Times. [online] Available at: http://www.nytimes.com/2014/11/15/business/keeping-a-vigilant-eye-on-pay-equity-for-women.html

163 Heidrick & Struggles International, Inc. 2020, Board of the Future. https://www.heidrick.com/en/insights/boardsgovernance/board of the future moving toward a more diverse more in tune european board